# Stolen Identity

Mary Louise

© Copyright 2021 – Mary Louise; All rights reserved.

Scripture quotations marked (KJV) are taken from the King James Version of the Bible.

Scripture quotations marked (NIV) are taken from the Holy Bible, New International Version®, NIV®. Copyright © 1973, 1978, 1984, 2011 by Biblica, Inc.™ Used by permission of Zondervan. All rights reserved worldwide. www.zondervan.com The "NIV" and "New International Version" are trademarks registered in the United States Patent and Trademark Office by Biblica, Inc.™

Scripture quotations marked (NKJV) are taken from the New King James Version®. Copyright © 1982 by Thomas Nelson. Used by permission. All rights reserved.

Scripture quotations marked (NLT) are taken from the Holy Bible, New Living Translation, copyright ©1996, 2004, 2015 by Tyndale House Foundation. Used by permission of Tyndale House Publishers, Inc., Carol Stream, Illinois 60188. All rights reserved.

Printed in the United States of America

ISBN 978-1-7375710-2-5

# Contents

| | |
|---|---|
| Introduction | 5 |
| 1. The Importance of Your Name | 7 |
| 2. Makeup | 13 |
| 3. Other Physical Alterations | 21 |
| 4. Head Covering | 31 |
| 5. 7 Days Without Wearing a Head Covering | 43 |
| 6. To Shave or Not to Shave? | 47 |
| 7. Rest | 59 |
| 8. Getting Rid of the Old | 65 |
| 9. Prosperity | 69 |
| 10. Prophecy | 79 |
| 11. There's Something About Water | 83 |
| 12. Does What We Wear Matter? | 91 |
| 13. First Fasting Experiences | 97 |
| 14. 40 Days On Water Only? | 105 |
| 15. Breaking the Fast | 125 |
| 16. Insurance | 133 |
| 17. 401(k) | 143 |
| 18. 501(c)(3) | 147 |
| 19. Wrap-Up | 151 |
| Prayer for Salvation | 153 |
| Other titles by this author | 155 |

# Introduction

I spent many years of my life trying to be what I thought the world and others found acceptable. I was trying to present what I thought others wanted to see. Magazine covers and movies had told me what was supposedly "beautiful" or acceptable. I also had accepted without question many other things that my parents, siblings, or others were doing.

Some might call what I was presenting to the world a "false" version of myself – something that I was trying to be, not something that I was created to be. I tried hard to avoid any more rejection in my life, but that false version of myself only brought more heartache and more pain into my life. My true identity had been stolen from me without me even realizing it.

Have parts of your true identity been stolen from you? As you read this book, you may discover that the answer to that question is yes.

I accepted many things in my life without question. If most everyone else seemed to be doing something, then I assumed that it was ok and that I should too. How many of you know that even large groups of believers have had parts of their identity stolen? How many Christians have been living bound for years? I was very bound for many years as a Christian.

After doing what most everyone else had done for many years and still ending up bound, lacking joy, and not walking fully in my true gifts and callings, God gave me hunger for truth – deep truths that would set me free. The Lord has changed my mind and renewed it in many areas. Romans 12:2 says to not be conformed to this world, but rather to allow the Lord to transform your mind. God continues to renew my mind. Through this book, God wants to renew your mind and to change your mind about some things. He wants to set you free and see you walk in all that He created you to be and do.

If you had told me 10 years ago that I would believe what I believe and know now, I might have thought you were crazy. I was bound, and God had to bit by bit set me free.

This book is a true account of my personal journey of getting free. There are things that are affecting us that God has changed my mind about. Some of these topics include makeup, shaving, clothing, retirement plans, and much more.

I encourage the men to read all of the chapters even if it doesn't seem like it applies to you. As leaders, husbands, and brothers, it's important for you to know how the enemy has been negatively affecting the women in your life.

I pray that God will now open the eyes of your understanding. I pray that He will give you the spirit of wisdom and revelation that Paul talks about in Ephesians. "I keep asking that the God of our Lord Jesus Christ, the glorious Father, may give you the Spirit of wisdom and revelation, so that you may know him better" (Ephesians 1:17, NIV).

Today, you are at a crossroads. "This is what the Lord says: 'Stop at the crossroads and look around. Ask for the old, godly way, and walk in it. Travel its path, and you will find rest for your souls' " (Jeremiah 6:16a, NLT). The Lord is wanting you to stop at this crossroads. There is an old, godly way that will give you rest for your soul.

Do you have great rest in your soul? Will you choose the old, godly way, regardless of what others are doing or not doing? The gate that leads to life is a narrow one, and few find it (Matthew 7:14, NKJV).

I pray that you will not be like the people in Jeremiah's day. The last part of the verse that talks about the crossroads says, "But you reply, 'No, that's not the road we want' " (Jeremiah 6:16b, NLT)! My prayer for you is that this will not be said of you. My desire is that you will reply, "Yes, that is the road we want. If the Lord says that this is the path that will give me great rest for my soul, then I choose to take it. I trust Him, His goodness, and His unfailing love."

I don't miss the broad path that kept me bound, insecure, and not fulfilling my destiny. I don't miss my true identity being stolen. The narrow path – the old, godly way, has brought me so much freedom, life, and joy. I now have taken back my true identity, and I have faith that you will too.

# 1
## The Importance of Your Name

What is in a name? Do you believe that your name is important?

Growing up, I hated my middle name – Louise. I never wanted anyone to know what it was. It was as though it was my biggest secret. I was ashamed of it and felt embarrassed by it. I can't really tell you how I came to hate it so much, as I don't remember anyone making fun of it, but I did think that it sounded very old-fashioned.

Is there any part of your name that you don't like? Do you know what your name means? I didn't know what my name meant until I was in my thirties.

As God freed me in many areas, He began to show me the importance of my name. He led me to look up the meaning of my first name and my middle name. I was able to identify strongly with each meaning.

My middle name, Louise, that I used to hate so much means "famous in war." How awesome is that? I'm not ashamed of it any longer, and I now accept, own, and love it completely, which is why it's on the cover of this book.

Your name is also significant. What does your first name mean? If you don't know, simply type in your internet search bar "meaning of name _____." If you are unable to access the internet, ask someone else to look it up for you.

It really doesn't matter if we like the sound of something; it matters what it means and how that is connected to who God created us to be. Warrior: that is totally me.

Warriors aren't afraid to go on the front lines in battle against their greatest enemies. That's another reason that I write this book – to come against Satan and his demons that have been deceiving people and stealing their identities from them. It's time to get back your true identity!

I wasn't able to understand any of this about my name and my identity when I was in bondage, trying to please people in the world that I didn't know well and that probably didn't even care about me.

This is one of many areas of breakthrough into my true identity and destiny. I want you to receive this breakthrough too, so I loose it to you now.

# Stolen Identity

I've known many people that are called something other than their true name, and often, I believe that it is an attack against their true identity. I've known a Daniel that was called "Danny." Danny wasn't in the lion's den; it was Daniel. Some people allow others to call them a shortened version of their name or even a nickname that doesn't reflect at all their true name or their true identity. I've also known Matthews that allow or even prefer that others call them "Matt." Matt wasn't one of the disciples, but Matthew was. It's important what people call us and what we hear over ourselves. It matters what we allow others to speak over us. I've also known Michaels that go by "Mike." Mike isn't an archangel, but Michael is.

What are others calling you? Is that your true name and your true identity? Are you insecure about your true name? Insecurity isn't from God. Are there bad memories from your childhood that have caused you to separate yourself from what you were called as a child? God wants to heal those areas now.

I just left the bank. The man who helped me was named "Bryanth." I asked him if he knew what his name meant. He didn't, so I looked it up. I didn't see the exact spelling, but "Bryant" means "strong." When I told him what his name meant, he said, "That is so me!"

God knew what He was doing when He directed our parents in naming us. Even if our parents didn't stop and ask God what to name us, God had a huge part in it.

It's so awesome to discover how our identity, gifts, and personality are connected to our names. It brings me great joy when I'm able to share this revelation with others and tell them what their name means.

You are here on purpose. Your life has purpose. Even your name is significant. You are significant. The enemy of our souls doesn't want us to know these things, but his time is about up, and I'm here to help you discover and uncover who God made you to be. No more stolen identity! We are taking back everything that has been stolen from us regarding our identity, especially our names. I hope that you're excited; I am!

Have you ever paid attention to the brand names of clothing or other items that you purchase? There's a clothing brand named "No Boundaries." I don't want anything on my body stating that I have no boundaries. I've also seen a nail polish called "Sinful Colors." Why would any believer want to put something on that has that in its name?

There's no need to invite demonic activity or temptations into our lives, which is exactly what these things in the natural can do. They open doors. The devil tries to be slick. He doesn't want us to be aware of his schemes and strategies, but please pay attention to names and labels. You might be surprised at what you are putting on you through clothing or other products.

The same is also true for food and drinks. Do you want to put a drink in your body called "Monster?"

The names of places are also significant. Be cautious where you decide to live. Look up the meaning of the city name and the street name before you move anywhere. Of course, be led by God in all of these things.

My childhood and early adult years in Memphis, Tennessee, USA, were very painful, as I was in great spiritual bondage. After moving to the state of Georgia and experiencing a lot of healing and deliverance, I started referring to Memphis as my "Egypt," meaning that it was my place of bondage. In Biblical times, the Israelites were enslaved by Egypt, so I connect bondage with Egypt.

I didn't realize at first that there was an actual city called Memphis in Egypt. That was wild when I discovered that. My experiencing a lot of bondage in a city that has the same name as a major city that was in Egypt is not a coincidence.

Crime rates are also no coincidence. Memphis, Tennessee, where I lived from approximately the age of 3 until my 30th year, had very high crime rates for many years. Pay attention to crime rates. These are indicative of high volumes of demonic activity in a particular area.

Basically, I lived in one of the darkest areas of the United States for more than 25 years. Yet, I thank God for those years. Once, I was bound, but now, I am free. And I will help others get free too. Nothing has to be wasted. Whatever the enemy intended for evil, God intends for good in our lives (Genesis 50:20).

I didn't notice the darkness of that area when I was living there. It was all I had known, so I was comfortable in it. I was spiritually bound. It was only after I moved away from that area and had much breakthrough that I realized the darkness of that area. When I returned to visit, I could sense the darkness as I drove into the area.

Have you looked up the meaning of your name? Allow yourself to be blessed as you unlock another part of who you are and why you're here. Also, look up the meaning of the name of your city. And please pay attention to brand names of the things that you buy.

There are times when God gives some a new name. Abram, Sarai, Jacob, and Simon are all great examples in Scripture. God renamed them to Abraham, Sarah, Israel, and Peter.

In the months that I was writing this book, a man of God singled me out in a service and asked me what my name was. At that time, my legal name was Sharon. That was the name that my earthly parents had given me. So, I told him my birth name of Sharon. He said that he might call me something different, something easier to remember, like "Mary." I smiled and wanted to be respectful, but I didn't think too much about it.

The next month, I was visiting the state of Kentucky in the USA. There was a prophet that was ministering to the people. I went forward for her to pray and prophesy over me. She said, "I don't know what your name is, but I keep hearing the name 'Mary, Mary'."

Then, in the next few months, I had two other people say that I remind them of "Mary." I always considered it a compliment as there are several Mary's in the Bible, but I didn't think too much about it.

At the time, I had already written most of this book that you are now reading, but I still needed to go back through and check for anything that needed to be edited or corrected. As I was reading and editing this chapter, God spoke to me and asked me how many times I needed to hear "Mary" before I would understand that He was giving me a new name and calling me to change my name.

I was shocked. I liked my birth name, "Sharon." I liked what it meant, and I connected a lot with its meaning. But I also sensed that I wouldn't be able to walk in all that God has for me unless I was obedient and received this new name.

God then reminded me that it was always a good thing when He changed someone's name, and it was part of their

## The Importance of Your Name

destiny. Abraham, Sarah, Israel, and Peter all had significant roles in the earth. They were God's instruments. I also am God's instrument. When God changes your name, it's not a downgrade, it's an upgrade.

So, I chose to obey God, and I legally changed my name to Mary. This has been very recent, so I can't tell you much except that I know it's good when God changes your name.

By the way, this wasn't a difficult thing to do in the United States. I got on the internet and researched how to do this. Then, I simply went to my county court's office, filled out a form, paid a fee, and waited to receive the court order with the judge's approval.

It wasn't hard. It simply takes time to find out what the process is and then do it. Then, I followed through with using that document from the court to get my name changed on everything else. And now, I am Mary. God truly makes all things new.

There are no examples in Scripture of anyone's identity or name being changed from one gender to another. You came into this world the gender that God intended you to be, and He makes no mistakes. You are not a mistake. Your gender is not a mistake. If you struggle in this area, call out to Jesus. He is eager to help you and bring healing and clarity into your life.

And if you are divorced, did you keep your ex-husband's last name? Do you want to still be known as that person's other half? If you kept his last name, that is exactly what your name is proclaiming. If you kept his name, you are keeping yourself tied to that person and tied to an identity of being that person's spouse.

What is God speaking to you about your name? Are there any changes that He wants you to make? Are you holding on to physical things from your past that are connected to an old name and an old you?

You are not an accident. You are extremely important and valuable. God had thoughts about you before the time of creation. He knew your name before you were ever born. He loves you so much.

What does your name mean? Are you living out your name's meaning? Are you living in your true identity?

Has God given you a new name? Have you fully embraced

it? What is He asking you to do now?

As you receive this blessing, pass it on. Look up what someone else's name means and share it with them. You might make their day and change their life.

Not accepting all of my name and not understanding its significance weren't the only things that had stolen from my true identity.

# 2
# Makeup

I started wearing makeup as a young teenager. I had two older sisters who wore makeup, and, of course, I wanted to do what the older girls were doing. Also, from a young age, I had played with Barbie® dolls who had their faces painted. Women on television and on magazine covers also wore makeup.

Although I didn't realize it, I was being told as a child what was beautiful, and a natural face wasn't what these images were telling me was beautiful. It's like I was being programmed by all of the images that I saw. What child doesn't want to "grow up" and do what the older ones and popular ones are doing?

I also had some acne as a teenager, and, of course, I wanted to cover that up. I was brutally made fun of in the seventh grade when I had a large pimple on my nose. It didn't matter how often I cleaned my face or what I treated it with, this one pimple seemed to stay forever.

I remember first putting "foundation," a liquid material, on my face. This is often put on the entire face. Then, I put powder on top of the foundation. This helped keep the foundation from melting, running, or smearing. I also began using mascara on my eyelashes. Then, I put lipstick on my lips. I also would sometimes wear eye shadow on the top of my eye lids.

Although that may sound like a lot, I didn't think that I wore a lot of makeup compared to some others that I knew. The foundation and powder were the main things that I wore, as these two items seemed to cover up or smooth out any "imperfections," discoloration, or anything else. I rarely wore mascara, as I quickly learned that this irritated my eyes, especially with my wearing contacts.

My normal day began with me putting on foundation, powder, and lipstick. On occasion, I would wear some eye makeup too. I suppose that I assumed that I looked better with it on. At some point, I began to feel that I couldn't be seen without the makeup on my face, as I perceived that it made me look better and "fixed" whatever I started to perceive needed fixing.

Once a person starts to do something, and it becomes a habit, that thing can strongly attach to the person. It can seem difficult to undo that thing that has become a part of one's daily life, particularly for years or even decades. Of course, Jesus can free a person in an instant.

It wasn't until I was approximately 30 years old that I realized that I had a problem with makeup. At this point, there were more years of my life that I had been wearing makeup than those that I hadn't.

I was driving to work one morning in 2012 in Savannah, Georgia. When I reached into my purse for my lipstick, I couldn't find it. I felt very panicked. I never went to work or anywhere else without lipstick on. In that moment, God showed me that feeling panicked without lipstick was evidence that there was a problem.

Did I think that people would treat me differently if I didn't have lipstick on? Did I think that people would reject me without it? Did I think that I looked that much different or was a different person with lipstick on? Why was I feeling so panicked?

This was early in my breakthrough season with the Lord. I was coming out of deep sin and spiritual bondage. I was going from death to life.

At that time, God and I had an agreement that I would give up or not do certain things for at least 7 months. One big one was not communicating with the married man that I had been in a relationship with before I moved to Savannah.

Although I had moved more than 600 miles away from that man and my former home, I had a strong soul tie with him, and it wasn't easy to break off communication. That was one of several things on my list for those seven months. Of course, I didn't plan to contact him after the 7 months either, but it's good to have a measurable goal when you're trying to get free in any area.

I was halfway through the 7 months when this moment with the lipstick happened. Who knew that lipstick could affect a person and the way that they think about themselves so much? This had happened without me even realizing the way that it was affecting me. God showed me that there was a problem. I added lipstick to my list of things to do without for those 7 months.

Not wearing lipstick was liberating. No one treated me any

differently when I didn't wear it.

That moment of panic regarding lipstick was my first sign that there might be a problem regarding my relationship with makeup. There was still much more to come.

When the seven months ended, I did wear lipstick again. But then, I found that my face was pretty clear, and I found myself sometimes only wearing lipstick and no other kind of makeup.

Over a period of time, I came to wear less and less makeup. This happened over approximately three years of me walking with the Lord. It was not overnight.

I need to testify about the power of Jesus right here. Not only did I not have any communication with that man for those 7 months, but it has now been over 9 years since I communicated with him! Have you ever been bound by something and weren't able to get free on your own? That was me regarding that relationship so long ago, but the power of God set me free! There's power in the blood of Jesus! Who the Son sets free is free indeed.

This is why I have a testimony and know the Lord so well. It's personal to me. Not only did He free me from that, but as I yielded to Him, He freed me from many other things, which you will read about.

In 2015, God called me to go on a mission trip to Brazil. Before I went, God said to me, "The less adornment, the more of my glory they will see." "Less adornment" – hmm, those are words that you never hear in our culture. I knew immediately what God was saying to me. Basically, I didn't need to wear anything that would draw attention to me in any way. He didn't have to explain; I knew in my spirit what this meant. I knew that I wasn't to wear any makeup or jewelry. I also knew that I needed to make sure to not wear anything that would draw attention to my figure in any way.

I wasn't going to Brazil to draw attention to me. I should be pointing people to Jesus. My desire was that the people would see Jesus, more so than me.

I didn't pack any makeup or jewelry for this trip. Thankfully, God had already been preparing me for this by having me wear less and less makeup.

By this point, there were days during the week at work

when I wore no makeup. In time, there were more days that I didn't wear makeup than those that I did. And guess what? The world did not come to an end when I didn't wear makeup.

This wasn't my first trip to Brazil. I had gone the previous year also, but I didn't get this word from God before that trip. Maybe I wasn't ready for it. God is so good. He's so gracious with us and helps us right where we're at. I love Him.

The first time that I went to Brazil was great, but let me tell you about some of the feedback that I got the second time when I wore no makeup and no jewelry. One woman came up to me and typed into her phone these words: "The love of God on your face!" Without saying a word, people could see the love of God on my face! I never heard anything like that the previous year when I was wearing makeup and jewelry.

There's something very profound and powerful about a person in their natural, God-given state. There's a beauty and a glory from within that emanates and is able to shine forth.

"But we all, with unveiled face, beholding as in a mirror the glory of the Lord, are being transformed into the same image from glory to glory, just as by the Spirit of the Lord" (II Corinthians 3:18, NKJV).

Makeup acts as a veil. This Brazilian woman had been around me the previous year when I was wearing makeup and had made no comments about "the love of God on your face." When I wore no makeup, she was able to see God emanating through me. "So God created man in His own image; in the image of God He created him; male and female He created them" (Genesis 1:27, NKJV).

I have known women who get up earlier than their spouse so that their husband will not see them without makeup on. I have also heard Christian women apologize for being seen without makeup on. I have known countless women who feel ashamed and insecure to be seen without makeup on. This is a problem!

It is not God's desire or design for anyone to feel ashamed of who He made them to be. It is terrible that so many women are not secure or confident in their natural state.

Makeup does not help anyone feel better about themself. It actually makes the person more and more insecure. I am speaking from experience. The more a woman wears makeup, the more she is agreeing with a lie that she is not good enough and not beautiful enough on her own.

I don't think that the majority of men have understood how much makeup can negatively affect a woman's self-image and self-esteem. This is changing.

There are two Christian men that I respect in many ways. They are both older and have much humility and wisdom in many areas. However, I heard both of them say something regarding makeup and their wives that pained me greatly for their wives.

One said how much he appreciates when the women take good care of themselves by wearing makeup, etc. Taking good care of themselves? Wearing makeup is not taking care of one's self. Showering and wearing clean clothes can be categorized as taking care of one's self, but wearing makeup is not equivalent to taking good care of one's self. Then, the other man half-jokingly said to a world-wide audience that he has seen his wife without makeup on and that he told her to never leave the house without it on.

I can guarantee you that these women are twice as insecure after being told these things by their own husbands, their other half, who should love the true and natural them more than anyone else does.

So, unfortunately, many men have also been programmed and brainwashed by images that they've been bombarded with.

Sadly, these mindsets and ways of thinking have been accepted and adopted by many Christians. I was at a Christian conference on relationships, where I learned some great things. But when the woman who was teaching mentioned a concept of hygiene and taking care of one's self, she had makeup on her list of ways that women can take care of themselves. This is so frustrating to me! What are these people teaching? It's time to get unbrainwashed!

God wants His children to be free! Jesus paid too high of a price for us to be walking around insecure and needing to alter and edit so many things about our God-given, outer appearance.

The last time that I wore makeup was in the fall of 2016, over five years ago. It's been so liberating. The next time that I dated, it was so wonderful to have met someone in my natural state with no makeup or jewelry on. To start that way – not being "made up", not trying to impress, and not feeling that I needed to alter my appearance in any way – was such a great feeling.

Unfortunately, many women, even married ones, do not feel secure or confident without adding to or altering their appearance in a variety of ways. I have compassion for them. I was one of them for many years.

I was extremely insecure. I didn't know my worth. I didn't know that I had something very valuable on the inside of me that far outweighs anything external. I only seemed to know what the world wanted to see from me externally, and I was good at presenting that to them.

Even as I re-read this portion, God is revealing that it's no coincidence that the first item of makeup that I used to put on, as do many women, is called "foundation." We don't need any foundation other than the one God has already given us. Your natural face is beautiful. You were perfectly and uniquely designed.

Strangely, many friends and family members do not even know what their loved ones truly look like. Many have been seeing a "made-up" image for so long that they don't even know what the true person looks like in their God-given state. Makeup allows a person to literally "make up" whatever image that they want to present to the world.

One man told me that he recently saw his adult sister without makeup on, and he almost didn't recognize her. This is the extent to which some women are altering their appearance through makeup. This is the extent to which makeup has been used to steal from a person's true identity.

Women are not the only ones that Satan wants to feel insecure. I realize that there are even some men who wear makeup, particularly those who are actors or who are on television. They also are allowing their God-given image and glory to be veiled or covered.

Attacks against our God-given image are also attacks against our Creator, as we are made by Him and in His image. Not only does Satan hate us, but he especially hates the One who created us, the One whose image we reflect when we leave ourselves in our God-given state. Satan is particularly jealous of the glory that we carry.

Satan doesn't want us to know what we carry. He also wants us to believe that something is wrong with our God-given faces so that we will alter them and cover them up. He is a deceiver and a liar.

If we were supposed to have a different color on our lips, then God would have made them that way. If God wanted our eyelids painted, then He would have painted them. God makes no mistakes. Nothing about your face is a mistake or can be done better through artificial things such as makeup, tattoos, or cosmetic surgery. Satan cannot make better what God Himself made.

What is God speaking to you now? What change is He calling you to make? Who is not able to see the love of God on your natural face?

After I stopped wearing makeup, I discovered that there was still a lot more that was stealing from my identity, confidence, and self-image.

# 3

## Other Physical Alterations

Playing with Barbie® dolls as a child, I was receiving the message that the image of this doll was what beautiful looked like. The doll's figure, hair color, painted face, and skin color were all shaping my ideas of what I thought that I should look like.

How many people do you know that naturally look like a Barbie® doll? Girls and boys are being bombarded with unrealistic images of what supposed beauty is from a young age. Barbie® dolls set up young girls to not feel good enough or pretty enough when they don't look anything like the doll. Girls start altering themselves in an effort to look "beautiful" or more like the doll. Many of us have been brainwashed.

I had no idea that my self-image and confidence were being negatively impacted by playing with Barbie® dolls. Many parents haven't realized this and have perpetuated the problem with their children. Seeing Barbie® dolls is not healthy for a young girl's or a young boy's perception of what beauty is.

Ironically, I was told more than once as a teenager that I looked like "Barbie." I had learned well what the world wanted to see from me, and I had worked very, very hard to present that to people.

When I was a teenager, I would lay outside in the sun for hours and hours to get a tan. I got severely sunburnt on more than one occasion. In the U.S., people seemed to like tanned skin on Caucasian people. I was good at presenting that, even at a great cost to myself.

In India, where shades of brown skin are more common, there has been a wide perception that lighter skin is better. There's a huge market for skin lightening products in India. In the U.S., there's a huge market for tanning beds and making one's skin appear darker.

Basically, whatever you are, the world and the devil want you to be dissatisfied with the way that God made you. There are beliefs and mindsets that have people spending lots of time and money trying to look different than the way that God made them.

It angers me now to recount all of this. I spent so much of

my life worrying about the exterior and spending time and energy trying to look like what I believed others wanted to see from me. And, for what? What did the world or any of those people ever do for me?

Sadly, some of us experienced so much rejection from our own parents or others that we couldn't seem to handle any additional rejection. This is why we worked so hard to not be rejected by the world at large.

Let's look at ourselves in the mirror in our most natural state for a definition of beauty. A good example is when you first get out of the shower. This is what the Creator of the universe thought was "very good" (Genesis 1:31). Everything else God made was "good," but after He made male and female, He said that what He saw was "very good."

It's time that we start believing God and what He says about us. He loves us and sent Jesus for us. We need to listen to His thoughts about us over these demonic images and ideas in the world. Those things are meant to steal from our true identity and our confidence.

God doesn't think that you need a different eye color, different hair, or different skin. He doesn't think that you need a different nose, different eyes, a different face, or a different body. He doesn't think there is anything wrong with your height.

There is nothing wrong with you. You are beautiful. You are beautiful without changing anything about yourself. Do you believe this? I want you to say out loud, "I am beautiful." Do you believe that you are beautiful without changing or modifying anything about yourself? I want you to say out loud, "I am beautiful in my natural, God-given state."

If someone made fun of you as a child or as an adult, where is that person now? Are they still in your life? Do they love you?

Don't allow what one or two people said about you to continue to bring you down. That is ending now. Often, people put others down to help themselves feel better about themselves.

Those people were probably unknowingly being used by the devil. Don't allow the devil and his thoughts to define you. He is a liar, and he wants to destroy you.

Those people also may have been jealous of you. The devil

## Other Physical Alterations

is jealous of the greatness that God has put inside each of us. If he can get people to feel bad about themselves, especially regarding their looks, he can get them bound in lies and struggling to be confident in their true identity and in what God has put inside of them. That is one of his objectives: to get us insecure, so that we spend our lives trying to be and look like someone else that God did not make us to be. Satan doesn't want you knowing your true identity, but it's time to believe and walk in what God says about you.

You are chosen. You are loved. You are not a mistake. You are beautiful. You are a masterpiece. You are wanted. You are amazing. You are God's child. You are God's creation, and He makes no mistakes. You have a Father, and He is good.

Although I never had an official eating disorder, I remember being conscious of staying thin as a teenager. I knew that I shouldn't get "overweight" based on all of the images that I saw on television, magazines, etc. I didn't always eat enough because of insecurity and fear of more rejection. I also remember getting a number stuck in my head, and that was the weight that I wanted to weigh. I would eat less to try to get to or stay under that number on the scale. Where did that number and that thought that I needed to weigh that amount or less come from? I now know that it was from the devil.

This whole thing is so frustrating. I'm frustrated to see how many people spend a large portion of their lives focused on the external. Satan loves when he gets us insecure and not knowing who we are. If he is able to do that, people then spend much of their lives trying to present something different on the exterior than their natural, true self. Meanwhile, they're not fully aware of the greatness inside of them. There's been so much wasted time but no more. I hope that you will say out loud as you read this, "No more, Satan; no more."

Hair is another huge topic. Growing up, I had long, straight, medium blonde hair. I used to get compliments on my long blonde hair. As I got older, it seemed to get darker. I now also wonder if the birth control "medicine" that I was on during part of my 20's changed my hair. Birth control messes with one's natural, God-given hormones, so I wouldn't be surprised.

Anyhow, I had never had a permanent, colored my hair, or altered my hair in any other long-term or drastic way up until the age of 29. A permanent is when curls or waves are added to or removed from a person's hair through the use of chemicals. In this season, I was in deep sin in a relationship with a married man. I was in great deception. Although this man had never said anything negative regarding my hair, for some reason, the thought came to me that I would look even better if my hair was like it used to be (a lighter shade of blonde, like when I was growing up). So, I decided to get my hair colored for the first time.

One of my coworkers got her hair colored quite often. I asked her where she went and then made an appointment at the same place. I remember saying when I got there, "It's just hair; what's the worst that could happen?" Bad, bad mistake. Never say, "What's the worst that could happen?"

It was a total disaster. First, the girl dyed it, and it turned out a brassy, orangish color instead of medium blonde. Then, she told me that my hair "pulled red," which actually looked like a brassy orange, and that the only way to get rid of the "red" was to bleach it. So, first, my pure hair was dyed; then, it was bleached. And in the end, it looked horrible. I felt ashamed after she got done with my hair.

I didn't feel ashamed before I went in; but afterwards, I felt very ashamed. And I PAID to have this done to myself! I left the place in tears and didn't want to be seen by anyone afterwards. Not only did I not get the results that I wanted, but I also lost what I originally had in the process.

This is called deception. Where did this thought come from about me looking better if I changed my hair to a lighter shade? The devil is where. The devil goes after hair. I can't fully explain it, but it's true.

Scripture says that a woman's long hair is a glory to her (I Corinthians 11:15, NKJV). Satan wants to take that glory from her. He doesn't only go after women though; he goes after men too. Just look around at how many people don't have their natural, God-given hair color or texture. The devil loves to strip our true identity and glory from us in any way that he can. He often does this through deception, criticism, and rejection.

Over a period of time and after going multiple places, I eventually got a color closer to the one that I had originally wanted. I continued coloring my hair for approximately three years.

Then, after experiencing much spiritual breakthrough and healing, God spoke to me and said that once my natural hair color grew back fully, I would have another breakthrough in my life. My hair was long. I asked the person who cut my hair how long she thought that it would take for my hair to fully outgrow the unnatural coloring. The answer was three years!

Isn't it amazing that we can lose something in a few minutes that will take three years to get back? The devil tries to be slick, but I am here to expose him! No more, Satan; no more!

I'm thankful to say that the last time that my hair was altered with any unnatural coloring was in 2014. My natural color is fully back, and I'm free of all of the fake coloring and everything that came along with it. My full glory is back. I took back what the devil had stolen.

Hair coloring and hair altering bring shame onto a person. Even when a person gets exactly what they want the first time they alter their hair, is this a good thing? If a person believes that their natural hair color or texture isn't good enough and they pay to keep changing it, is this healthy? Is this God's design? Just like with makeup, the longer a person agrees with the lie that they are not good enough without the alteration, they get more and more bound. They are in agreement with a false version of themselves, which actually keeps their confidence and self-esteem low.

There's something spiritual about hair. Samson in the Bible had a special anointing and strength that was connected to his hair (Judges 13-16). The devil wants to steal our strength and our anointing.

I also find it interesting that during the Holocaust, one of the first things that the Nazis did to the majority of the people in the concentration camps was to shave their heads or cut their hair very short. They took their hair from them. Satan understands that there is glory associated with hair, and he loves to strip people of their God-given glory.

Sadly, many have been brainwashed into believing that what the world portrays as attractive is what must be attractive. Many believe that artificial blonde is attractive even on people to whom it clearly is not natural and does not go with their God-given skin tone.

I look around and see so many unnatural colors such as blue, purple, etc. Some people almost look like clowns with so much unnatural coloring on their faces and their hair. It's sad. I think that the devil loves it. He loves for people to be in deception, confusion, and self-rejection.

This is what people are doing as they alter themselves. They are rejecting themselves. The alteration doesn't help them feel better about themselves. It makes them feel worse. If someone likes them or accepts them more after the alteration, this only helps trap them further in the lie that they are not good enough or attractive enough in their natural, true self. That person is actually liking a false self.

Are you presenting your true self or a false self to the world? I was presenting a false self for many years.

Are you in a relationship with the true self of the person you are with or a false version of that person? Do you encourage the people in your life to be their true selves, or are you part of the problem?

This is why some men and some women struggle to come out of these things. They are afraid that the person they are with will not like them as much if they don't keep altering their appearance to make it what it was when they first met that person. This is sad, and it is not love if the person doesn't accept or like the true you.

I heard one man say that he had been married to many different women in his life. In reality, he had only been married to one woman, but he was referring to the many different changes she went through during their marriage.

Once a person begins altering himself or herself in any way, this seems to open a door for even further bondage. One is never happy or satisfied with the one alteration. After one comes into agreement with that lie of the devil that they weren't good enough to begin with, Satan will keep coming with other things that could be "fixed" or "better."

Look around. People aren't just painting a different color onto their fingernails; now, many are attaching fake nails. Women aren't just wearing mascara; some are now attaching fake eyelashes. People aren't only coloring their hair; sometimes, they are wearing someone else's hair. Whose hair

## Other Physical Alterations

and whose identity are on your head? Is that even human hair?

Some are spending thousands of dollars to alter their appearance through surgery. How many women have had false objects implanted into their breasts in order to make them look artificially larger? I am sure that there were other lies that they first came into agreement with before they took the step of surgery. And my heart goes out to them. They are clearly hurting and not feeling good about themselves to have gone through that.

I've heard of many surgery stories in which people have had similar experiences to what I had when I went to get my hair colored. Not only did I not get what I wanted or intended to get, but what I originally had was also lost in the process. I was in deception and was unknowingly yielding to a deceptive, demonic spirit. This has happened to many people when they go in for a cosmetic surgery.

Instead of coming out "better," they come out in even worse shape, having lost what they originally had and having paid to have it done! Rather than getting their supposed problem solved, they come out of the place with new problems. There's a television show dedicated to these horrible cosmetic surgeries that have "gone wrong." Of course, that was the devil's intent all along. The devil doesn't give us good things. He only wants to take from us. God is the giver of good things, and the things that God gives us don't steal from our true identity.

The devil is a liar. It's a sad cycle, but it's stopping now! If you agree, please say out loud, "It is stopping now!"

It can take time to untrain the brain. I didn't immediately see myself as beautiful when I stopped wearing makeup. I had unknowingly trained my own brain to think that artificial coloring on the face was much more attractive than what God had naturally put there. Of course, this was what I had seen for decades through Barbie® dolls, movies, magazines, and other people around me.

I struggled a few times after I had given up makeup and had thrown all of my makeup away. The devil tried to get me to go backwards and buy more makeup at the store on more than one occasion. The devil wants us to be bound, not free.

But, how could I go backwards? Why go backwards? Why

go back into bondage when Jesus paid such a high price for my freedom? Jesus wants us to know who we are, not to go around unsure and needing to try to be like everyone else. He doesn't want us to be anyone other than exactly who He created us to be.

There was an unspoken pressure that would try to come to me at times to try to get me to be like everyone else. Even in the Christian community, how many women wear zero makeup? Not enough, but this is changing.

The devil even tried to use a guy in my life to send me backwards. The guy said something like, "You never wear makeup or do anything with your hair." Those words were straight from the devil. The devil didn't like that he had lost his hold on me in these areas.

I was now in more of my true identity, and the devil hates when we accept ourselves and present our true selves to the world. By the way, I no longer allow that person in my life. It's important to cut people out of your life that don't love the true you and that the devil uses to try to bring you down. Of course, be led by the Lord in all of these things.

The very fact that the devil tried to attack this part of me confirms how powerful it is when we love ourselves and don't alter ourselves. If someone has attacked part of your true identity, let that confirm how wonderful and how powerful those parts of you actually are.

I want to implore the men to make a positive difference in this area. All of our words are powerful, but men, your words carry a special weight. We are still calling the animals the same names that Adam originally gave them.

Men, use your weight in words for good, not for evil. How can you encourage the women around you to be natural and who God made them to be?

When I was a teenager, I was at the grocery store with my friend and her boyfriend. He made a comment to her half-jokingly that she should "get a pair of those," referring to someone on the magazine cover that had large breasts. This causes me to fume even to this day. That is a horrible thing to say to anyone. I have no words to explain how this made me feel to hear that. This is an exact example of the devil speaking through someone into your life.

## Other Physical Alterations

How would he feel if his significant other told him that maybe he should get a bigger _____? These comments are lower than low, yet some people have the audacity to say them. What's worse is that this is what is in their hearts. "You brood of vipers, how can you who are evil say anything good? For the mouth speaks what the heart is full of" (Matthew 12:34, NIV). Shallow, artificial, and demonic are the words that come to my mind. Part of me still wants to slap that guy for what he said, and he didn't even say it to me.

If you watch pornography, you are filling your eyes and more importantly your heart with evil. When these types of things are in a person's words and heart, they have come from somewhere. God tells us to guard our hearts. "Guard your heart above all else, for it determines the course of your life" (Proverbs 4:23, NLT).

God is not behind pornography. The evil that enters one's heart through pornography will eventually hurt those closest to them, even if they are not yet married. Of course, Jesus can set you free and purify your eyes and your heart. If you struggle in this area, please call out to Jesus. He will help you. He overcame everything on the Cross. Nothing is too hard for Him.

I have heard of many people getting free from this after fasting for three days. They ate no food and were free after just three days.

This is another area of identity that the devil wants to steal from people. Much of what is being viewed and accepted through movies and pornography is not of God and leads to problems.

I once heard a Christian man probably in his 60's say, "There's nothing wrong with looking." Um, yes, there is something wrong with looking. King David, who was a man after God's own heart (Acts 13:22), looked at a woman without clothes on who was not his wife. His looking led to multiple people dying (2 Samuel 11-13).

Looking can lead to death, whether physical death or death of your God-ordained relationship. It has before, and it can again. Looking is serious. Guard your eyes and your heart for your spouse, whether you are married yet or not.

What is God speaking to you? What change does He want you to make today?

Do you love and accept your true self?

Are you helping those around you be their true selves, or are you hindering them from being who God made them to be?

Please don't ever criticize a person's natural appearance. That is how God made them. Please don't attack God's creation.

Be the person that God made you to be, and help others take back what the enemy has stolen in their lives too.

There was still a further revelation that I would need to walk in before I would truly see myself as beautiful. This next chapter is an important one and is the topic that I've received the most questions on.

# 4

# Head Covering

Some of you may have never heard these two words together: head covering. I hadn't heard of this until 2017, the year after I stopped wearing makeup.

I was listening to a Christian woman online. God led her to wear a headscarf. She mentioned feeling protected from the demonic realm and some other positive things. Eventually, she started wearing something on her head daily.

Initially, I didn't consider it for myself. As time went on though, God led me to search out the matter of head covering.

I started seeing women wearing head coverings. I knew that this was not a coincidence. I don't know if the women were Christian, Jewish, Muslim, or something else, but it didn't matter. I knew that these were signs from God.

In my research, I heard about one testimony from a group in Great Britain. There was an older woman who had held a women's Bible study in her home for years. One day, the woman died. The women in the group said to each other, "We believe in miracles; we know that God can raise her from the dead." So, they prayed for God to bring her back to life. Nothing happened, so the women went home. One of the women had a young son. When the woman mentioned what had happened, the son said, "Did you cover your heads while you prayed?" So, this woman called all of the women and told them to grab whatever they had to cover their heads.

The women covered their heads with hats, scarves, or whatever they had on hand and returned. The women prayed again for God to bring the woman back to life. This time, she came back to life! Sometimes, it's children that get the revelation!

I also listened to testimonies from men who have cast demons out of people. Some of these men have had conversations with the demonic spirits. One man said that a demon manifested and said that it "hates when women cover their heads." Why would demons care whether or not women cover their heads?

Derek Prince, a powerful man of God who is now with the Lord, operated strongly in deliverance ministry. If you watch any of his messages, his wife is in the audience with some kind of head covering on her head.

There's a passage in I Corinthians 11 that talks about head covering. It says that God is the head of Jesus, Jesus is the head of man, and man is the head of woman (verse 3). It says that a man who prays or prophesies with his head covered dishonors his head (verse 4). It also says that a woman dishonors her head if she prays or prophesies with her head uncovered (verse 5).

The more I searched, the more conviction that I felt about head covering. I would be sitting at my desk at work and would start talking to God. I felt like I needed to hold my hand over my head out of respect for God before I spoke to Him.

The conviction got stronger. When I was at home, I would grab a shirt, towel, or anything else nearby and put it on top of my head before I started talking to God. I didn't fully understand it, but I knew it was the right thing to do.

Although I was a lot freer than I used to be, I still had further to go. In this process, I learned that hair can provide a certain amount of feelings of "security," especially for women. Even if women aren't fully aware of how much glory is connected to their hair, on some level, they know that their hair is important and attractive. Hence, much time, products, and resources are often spent on hair.

I had always liked to wear my hair down and around my face. I felt that it looked best that way. Once I gave up makeup, I still had my hair that I was finding some kind of "security," identity, or self-worth in. I didn't realize any of this though until after I began to do the next thing that God put on my heart to do: wear a head covering.

It reached a point where I couldn't keep trying to hold my hand over my head at my desk every time that I wanted to talk to God. I like to talk to Him a lot throughout each day.

In preparation, I bought some scarves. There were a lot of helpful videos online that helped teach me how to wrap my hair and tie the scarf around my head.

On Sunday, October 29, 2017, I wore a head covering for the first time in public. I wore it to church. The scarf covered most of my hair with only some of my bangs out. I was not happy about wearing the scarf on my head. I didn't want people to stare at me or ask me questions. I just wanted to be left alone.

I knew that I was supposed to do this, but it was not easy. It felt extremely hard to do something that I knew would draw attention to myself. I hoped that no one would come and talk to me. I felt kind of angry or something that day.

The pastor's wife came and asked me if I was ok. I realized that I was sitting with my arms folded and feeling like I didn't want to be there. I don't know what all I was getting freed from, but getting free is not always fun in the process.

I couldn't wait to leave church that day. I went to the store afterwards, and the scarf kept slipping off my head. This frustrated me. There can be a lot of details to figure out when a person decides to cover their head.

What do I use? Do I cover all of my hair? What do I do with my hair underneath? What, if anything, do I tell others about this?

The first time that you do something is usually, by far, the hardest. The first day that I wore a headscarf in public was definitely the hardest. The next day was a work day.

I knew that if I was going to do this, I needed to do it every day. So, I wore a headscarf to work the next day. Again, I left a little bit of my bangs out on day two.

I realized that day that I found some comfort or security in having a little bit of my hair around my face. Once I realized that, I knew that I needed to cover it all. God doesn't want us mostly free. He wants us completely free. By day three, I was covering all of my hair.

Oh, the stares that I got at work! I could feel them from seemingly every angle. I just wanted to be left alone. Initially, I knew I was supposed to do this, but I couldn't have explained to anyone why, nor did I want to. It was hard enough to do it. Expecting anyone to understand or agree was definitely not an expectation that I had.

When I first started wearing a head covering, there was a lot of experimentation and learning as I found what worked and what didn't. I was in the initial stage, which I will call the awkward stage. This stage is: I am doing this in obedience to God, but it may look and feel awkward for various reasons.

I tried to avoid conversations with my coworkers as much

as possible in those first few weeks because I didn't want them asking me questions about the head covering. It took a full two weeks of me continually wearing a head covering before my coworkers seemed to understand that this was not a fad and that I would continue to have something on my head.

There was spiritual warfare surrounding this. I could feel one particular woman staring at me a lot. Another stopped me in the bathroom, said that a couple people had mentioned that I was acting strange, and bluntly asked me why I was wearing that.

God gave me great strength to handle these situations. I simply said, "It's kind of personal." She didn't press further and said that she assumed it was religious or something like that.

Some people are nosy or curious. Others are used by the devil to try to discourage you from the next level in your journey, particularly when it affects your identity and freedom. Still, others are used by God.

I noticed one woman looking at me, and I was praying that she would not stop by my desk and ask me any questions. I already had some remarks made to me such as, "Are you becoming a Muslim?" "Are you cold?" "Did you get a haircut?"

The woman that I didn't want to talk to came to my desk and directly asked me, "Why are you doing that?" I replied, "It's kind of hard to explain." She then said, "You don't have to. It takes a real strength to do what you are doing." I thought to myself, "You have no idea what it is taking for me to come in here with this on my head." Yet, her words expressed that, on some level, she did know how hard this was. She later told me that she has wanted to wear one to work in the past but never had.

I have found that the devil hates when we do bold things. He also hates when we get free in areas that hinder our confidence and our understanding of our identity. Satan will try to fight you and discourage you from doing what God calls you to do.

After being questioned by multiple people about why I was doing this and also hearing that a couple of people had mentioned me to a supervisor, I knew that what I was doing was powerful in the spiritual realm. Why else would people or the devil care what I was doing if it had no impact? Apparently, when a woman covers her head, it has great impact.

I have continued to wear a head covering since that time, and it has blessed my life tremendously. So many good things have happened. It's hard for me to now imagine not wearing something on my head. I've actually grown very fond of it; granted, that did take some time.

I was hearing from God before I wore a head covering, but after I started wearing one, I was amazed by how many more revelations and downloads that I got from the Lord.

I'm also treated with much more respect by men than I ever was before I started head covering. When I go to the grocery store or other places, men go out of their way to hold doors open for me and allow me to go first. I am now treated more like the royalty and the lady that I am than I ever was before I started head covering.

More than a year and a half after I started head covering, God showed me the reason that men respect me more. As I respect God's order of authority and wear something on my head, men are receiving more respect through me without me saying any words. They may not understand in the natural what is happening, but, on some level, their spirits sense the respect.

Let's go back to I Corinthians 11. God is the head of Jesus; Jesus is the head of man; and man is the head of woman (verse 3). God, Jesus, men, then women. Verse 7 says that men are the image and glory of God, and women are the glory of man. In verses 4-5, men dishonor their head (Jesus) if they pray or prophesy with their heads covered; women dishonor their head (men) if they pray or prophesy with their heads uncovered.

Conversely, when a woman covers her head when she prays or prophesies, she honors her head, which is man. So, a woman covers her head, which points back to the men. Men are the image and glory of God, so, as they leave their heads uncovered, they point back to their head, Jesus. Then, Jesus points back to God. It's quite beautiful, actually. The women cover their heads pointing back to the men, who leave their heads uncovered pointing back to Jesus. Jesus, who was sent by God the Father, points back to His Father. It all points back to God as the head of all.

I Corinthians 11:10, KJV, says that the woman should have "power on her head because of the angels." The NKJV translates that the woman should "have a symbol of authority on her head, because of the angels." The NLT says that "because the angels are watching, a woman should wear a covering on her head to show she is under authority." Although I don't have full revelation on this verse's meaning, apparently, women wearing or not wearing a head covering affects the angels. I'm assuming that this ties into why the demons hate when women wear a head covering.

Ultimately, when women cover their heads in obedience to God, they are pointing back to Him as the head of all and honoring His order of authority on the earth. I'm sure that demons hate when women proclaim through head covering that God is the head of all, not Satan.

Sometimes, I will catch a man looking at me, and it almost seems that he can't look away. It's not a natural or carnal attraction that he is drawn to; it's the glory of God.

I don't think that they know why they can't seem to look away. I know that some are curious or haven't seen this before, but there's much more to it than that. As I cover my glory, my hair, I am honoring God as the head of my life and pointing others to Him even if their minds don't comprehend it.

I don't need to show my own glory. I'm here for a far greater purpose than that. What an honor to get to point back to the Lord with this one simple act of obedience.

A woman wearing a head covering is powerful. When a person is in obedience to God, it is extremely powerful.

I am powerful; you are powerful; and we are even more powerful when we are free. When we get free of us and the world, we are better able to glorify God and fulfill our God-ordained purposes. Understanding and walking in this head covering revelation has freed me further.

Because I Corinthians 11:15, KJV, and NKJV, say that long hair is a glory to a woman and is a covering for her, some have thought that hair alone is the covering that this passage is referring to.

Let's assume that for a moment. Men, you should take your hair off in order to honor your head when you pray or prophesy. Huh? Women, you should put your hair on your head when you pray or prophesy in order to honor your head. How much sense would that make?

## Head Covering

Because this passage says that if a woman has long hair, it is a glory to her, I believe that this is part of why a woman covering her hair, her glory, helps point back to someone else. As women cover their glory, they point to a greater glory.

Hair is a type of covering, but if hair is the only covering that matters when we pray or prophesy, Paul, the writer of this book, would not have needed to mention what we should or should not be doing during those times. Clearly, our natural hair on our heads does not come off and get put back on at different moments that we decide.

Some questions that arise are: 1) How often should a woman wear a head covering? 2) Should she cover all of her hair? 3) Does this only pertain to when you are assembled with other believers for prayer, worship, etc.? 4) Does this apply to all women or only those that are married? Each person and family should seek God for themselves and do as He leads in each of these areas.

When God led me to begin wearing a head covering, I was unmarried. I have found that in any setting, when a woman wears a head covering to honor the Lord and His order of authority, it completely changes the atmosphere. I've seen it for myself.

Imagine if women were free enough to not need to show, style, or alter their hair or themselves. Imagine if men and women walked freely as God designed without trying to impress others and without altering or editing themselves in any way. Imagine if the people of God understood what they have on the inside of themselves and walked confidently because of that. Imagine not being bogged down with so much focus on the exterior that will soon pass away.

I don't spend any time, energy, or money on makeup or hair styling anymore. It's so wonderful! Freedom!

I didn't clearly see myself as God sees me after I gave up makeup, although I was closer than before. Only after I additionally started covering my hair did I begin to see myself as truly beautiful in my natural state.

When all other forms of "beauty" that the world had trained my mind and my eyes to see as beautiful were stripped away, I began to see, accept, and appreciate the real me as God designed. I was in my 30's before I really began to see myself as beautiful. How crazy is that?

What's even sadder is that there are many men and women all over the world who do not know who they are and do not see themselves as beautiful in their natural state. This is changing! It's time to take back what was stolen: our understanding, our vision, and our acceptance of our true, God-given identity. I believe that women will begin head covering all over the world.

I've had other experiences that have also confirmed the power of women wearing a head covering. Once, I was at a prayer night at my friend's church. God told me to give a woman there my headscarf. Underneath the outer headscarf, I was wearing a cotton cap that covered and held in all of my hair. So, I could give the scarf away and still have my head covered.

It felt awkward to take my outer headscarf off, but sometimes, it's best to intentionally feel awkward to make sure that you stay free and don't get insecure about anything.

After the service, I gave my headscarf to this woman that I had never met before. She put it around her neck and started immediately prophesying. She said, "I see you writing a book." I was writing my first book at that time. Then, she proceeded to tell me other things that were happening in my life.

Not too long after that, I was with another group of Christian friends at a coffee shop. Again, God told me to give my headscarf to a woman there, so I did. She put it on, and minutes later, she was prophesying to the whole group.

God showed me that it was not a coincidence that these women started prophesying once they put on the scarf that had been on my head. There's something really powerful about a woman covering her head. I hope you are getting this.

I've often been the only woman wearing a head covering in any given situation. Someone has to be first.

One woman who was incarcerated asked me about my head covering. I talked to her at length about it. Some people are genuinely interested, and God wants to bring them into the revelation. God gives wisdom regarding how much to share with each person.

I've had some women ask me about head covering with a judgement already made before they've listened. You can see the judgement on their faces and hear it in their voices. God says not to cast your pearls before swine (Matthew 7:6), so clearly, I don't share much with them.

I think that some women are convicted by my head covering, even if they don't understand it. Of course, how can a person understand something unless God reveals it to them?

The next time that I went to the prison, the woman whom I had talked at length with about head covering was eager to see me. She said, "I've got to talk to you!"

She looked to be in her mid-thirties. She was so excited to tell me that she had researched it, prayed about it, and knew that it was the right thing to do. She had also discussed it with her husband, who was totally fine with it. She let her family know that she would be doing this when she got out, which was soon. At that time, the prison did not allow her to cover her head in public areas. I told her that God saw her heart. She said that she was using an old shirt to cover her head when she prayed in her private dormitory. She told me that a couple of other women in her dorm had started doing the same.

I love when people get it! It is something that God has to reveal to a person, and I love when people are open to what God is saying and is wanting to do in their lives.

It used to be common for women to wear something on their heads in the house of God. In some parts of the world, it is still common. If you watch older movies, the women wore a hat or bonnet or something on their heads in church. Conversely, it has also been previously considered disrespectful for a man to wear a hat in God's presence.

Why is this? Where did this originate from? Although it's mentioned in I Corinthians 11, I believe that it goes back much further than that. I believe that it was part of the covering that was given by God to Eve after what happened with the serpent in the garden.

Only after I was free from makeup, hair coloring, and other things was I then able to get this revelation on head covering. I don't know that I could have learned about this subject first. This revelation is one of the most life-impacting revelations that I've ever received.

Sometimes, we can get spiritually stuck until we choose to act on what God has already shown us.

Stolen Identity

Anything that God has ever asked me to do or to give up has never been for Him; it's always been for me and for others, although I haven't always understood that in those moments. He knows what holds us back or prevents us from fully knowing who we are and why we are here on this earth.

It's amazing how many things from this world can get into us even while growing up in a supposedly "Christian" environment. I've been on a journey of getting unbrainwashed. Scripture calls this the renewing of our minds (Romans 12:2). Thankfully, God makes all things new (II Corinthians 5:17), especially our thinking.

I get tired of being around believers who aren't open to being different than the rest of the world. We are not here to be like everyone else. The Scriptures say that we are a peculiar people (Deuteronomy 14:2 and I Peter 2:9, KJV).

We are also the light of the world (Matthew 5:14). Light stands out and looks different than darkness. I spent too many years blending in with the world. That is not why we're here.

I hope that you hear my heart as you read this. This is not about condemnation. This is not about makeup or head covering. It's about freedom and identity. I want you to be free. I want you to know why you're here and to walk fully and confidently in your destiny and the purposes that God has for your life. I don't want Satan to get away with anything else. I want you to know who you are.

It's time for us to be smarter than the devil. It's time for us to be more than ok with not being like everyone else. What did the world or the people in it ever do for you anyway?

The more I walk in obedience to God, the more He reveals to me. I didn't know how powerful or life-changing head covering would be when I first started doing it. I believe that it was on the third day of my covering my head that I was able to get more revelation about it. Some things you will not understand until you actually do them.

I listened to a message, and the man mentioned that the angels in Scripture use their wings to cover themselves in the presence of the throne of God (Isaiah 6:1-3). This picture in my mind helped me to really understand this whole thing. The angels choose to cover themselves, to cover their own glory, as a way to point back to God and His glory. This greatly helped me in understanding what head covering does.

As John the Baptist stated, "He must increase, but I must decrease" (John 3:30, NKJV). There's still much more to learn on this, but I'm so thankful for what God has revealed thus far.

What is God stirring you to do right now? Is He asking you to give up something or to change something? Will you? Are you willing to let Him free you? You're going to feel great afterwards. The process may take some time, but it will be so worth it.

Although a lot of chapters of my first book were written before I started head covering, I couldn't seem to finish that first book. After I started head covering, I was able to take the next steps towards book publication. I don't know if I ever would have finished my first book if I hadn't started covering my head.

I've heard some women state that they have more clarity and are more productive when they wear a head covering. Head covering affects our identity and our destiny.

I definitely see myself more clearly and know my own value so much more after wearing a head covering, but what would happen if I stopped wearing a head covering?

# 5
# 7 Days Without Wearing a Head Covering

Twenty months after I began covering my head, a woman from church told me that God wanted me to stop wearing the hats that I had been wearing. She thought that I was "hiding" under the hats and that God didn't want me to hide.

I didn't feel that I was hiding. I simply found it easier to put a hat on my head than to tie a headscarf. I also enjoyed experimenting with different types of head coverings.

Although it wasn't said that I should totally not wear a head covering, I felt defensive, as I knew that head covering was something that God had called me to do.

It's important that we test anything that anyone brings to us. I asked the Lord what He wanted me to do, and He led me to test this matter out by not wearing anything on my head for 7 days. Although I had gone a day or so without a head covering, this would be the longest I had gone since October 2017 without covering my head.

How would I feel or act without wearing a head covering? Do I feel free without it? Jesus came to set us free after all.

Initially, it was very uncomfortable. Change can be uncomfortable. Also, I do have a sense of being covered and protected in not only the natural realm but more importantly in the spiritual realm when I have something on my head.

I recently heard about a man in another country. He had a female cousin get abducted by a man who intended to rape her. The man asked her to remove her head covering, and she refused. The head covering seemed to prevent him from being able to fulfill the evil that he wanted to do to her. He released her without harming her physically or sexually.

God told me that He had me and that I was still protected without covering my head for those seven days. It was hard to not want to cover my head when I prayed. Out of habit, I did initially put my hand there or grab a scarf when I began to pray, but then, God gave me peace about it. He knows my heart and that I honor Him as the head of my life.

Some people have stared at me; they've never seen my entire head and hair before. Some make a point to compliment my hair. They don't understand that I'm not ashamed of my hair. I don't cover my head or my hair because I don't like it.

Frankly, having my hair out has been more work. With my hair out, I've felt the need to wash it more frequently. My scalp and hair don't get as oily when I have my head covered. I also don't need to think much about combing or brushing my hair when it's wrapped and covered. It's a nuisance to have to think about my hair after not having had to think about it for so long.

Some people are more drawn to me physically or carnally with my hair out. I want people to be drawn to my face that emanates the Spirit of God that's inside of me, not my hair.

I found myself feeling comfortable without wearing a head covering within a few days, but I also missed my head covering. It's become a part of me. I love it. It's also connected me with so many people, particularly those of different nationalities and different spiritual backgrounds. In some countries, head covering for women is considered a form of modesty.

One of my female coworkers said that sometimes, she feels the need to wear something on her head so that she can "decrease." It's interesting that head covering is a way for a woman to decrease in order that Jesus can increase. How beautiful is that? "And I, if I am lifted up from the earth, will draw all peoples to Myself" – Jesus in John 12:32, NKJV.

Life isn't about me, and it's not about you. The created has the opportunity and privilege to point back to their Creator. There's a wonderful freedom when we know and understand that us being here isn't about us. We don't have to try to be anything or look any certain way or even have our hair out as women.

I'm trying to verbalize this subject of head covering for women, but some things have to be experienced. I feel more like me when I have a head covering on my head. There's something wonderful about forcing others to see you for you and not needing to show or draw attention to anything else. I don't need to wear makeup or jewelry. I don't need to fix my hair or even show my hair. I don't need to draw attention to my figure. I just get to be me, and it's such a wonderful thing.

If others don't like it, that's their prerogative, but why should I be less than who God has called me to be? Why should I conform to make others feel more comfortable or to appeal more to their eyes or flesh?

## 7 Days Without Wearing a Head Covering

Many in the body of Christ haven't understood why I do this, but I must stand my ground. One Christian woman told me that she thought that I would only do this for a season. I don't know fully what the future holds, but I don't see myself giving this up.

I did get rid of some of my hats, as I think that headscarves have a humility about them. Also, headscarves often allow others to see one's face better, and our natural faces reflect God.

My head covering journey has taken twists and turns. Sometimes, my head has felt itchy, or my hair has broken more when I've kept it wrapped in the same way all the time, so I allow my head to "breathe" and wear a different head covering and leave some hair out. I've also enjoyed throwing a hat on my head on some days and not having to tie a headscarf. If I'm going to be in direct sunlight for many hours, then I may choose a hat that day. The great thing is that there is freedom in this.

Although there is freedom for me to not wear a head covering all the time, I miss it when I don't wear one. I realize that I might look more "attractive" to some in the natural realm when I leave my hair out and basically choose to be like the world, but that's not who I am. That's not why I'm here. My value doesn't come from the external. I'm not here to draw people to the natural.

Head covering is a deep and personal journey. I hope that all women will choose to try this and experience the amazing things that God wants them to know through it.

Since I began head covering, I am more myself than I've ever been. I'm more confident than I've ever been. I'm more content than I've ever been. My focus is clearer than it's ever been. I'm freer than I've ever been. I'm so thankful that God led me to it. He is such a good Father!

Seven days without wearing a head covering confirmed that God has called me to this, and I love it!

Head covering hasn't been the only revelation that has completely changed my life for the better. Next, I began to wonder, "What's up with all of the shaving?"

# 6

## To Shave or Not to Shave?

In 2017, something started bothering me about shaving. I wondered, "Who thought this up, and why?" What is the purpose of shaving?

I learned that women haven't always shaved. For hundreds of years, women didn't alter their body hair in any way, and life continued just fine. So, why are women shaving now?

The world promoted shaving, along with images of women who shaved, through newspapers, magazines, and eventually, television and movies. And, of course, there were companies ready to take one's money for suddenly "necessary" shaving products.

The world portrayed images of women without hair in places that it normally would be. Suddenly, it was presented that it was unacceptable or unattractive to have hair under one's arms if you were a woman. Apparently, women came into agreement with those images.

The more I looked into shaving, the more it made zero sense to me why we shave. "Everyone else does" has stopped being a good enough reason for me to do anything.

I listened to some testimonials from women who experimented with not shaving. It always helps to hear from those who have courage to not conform to what the culture seems to expect. I'm thankful for those who have inspired me. I hope that these words will also give you great strength, inspiration, and boldness.

In November 2017, I decided to experiment with not shaving. I wasn't sure for how long I would do this, but fall was turning into winter, so it wasn't hard to just wear a long skirt or pants and not expose my "no shaving experiment." I was doing this for myself, not for anyone else.

At first, I hated seeing hair on my legs. My mind, my eyes, and my brain had been trained and programmed for decades with thoughts of: "Hair doesn't belong on a woman's legs," and "Hair on a woman's legs is ugly, gross, or negative." In my mind, only men were supposed to have hair on their legs. Why though? God put hair on women's legs too.

I had no memory of what my legs looked like before I

started shaving. I was around 11 or 12 years old when I started shaving my legs. Mainly, I remember wanting to do what the older girls were doing.

As soon as I shaved my legs that first time as a child, an immediate sense of shame seemed to come on me regarding me having hair in those places that it had always been (my legs and my underarms). I didn't have this shame before I began shaving. That hair had never bothered me before.

I don't know fully how this affected me at the time, but hair naturally grows in these places, so there was a continual need to "fix myself" and get rid of this hair that kept coming in. It was a constant source of insecurity if I hadn't freshly shaved my legs.

I can't count the number of times that I didn't feel comfortable to wear a certain thing or be seen at all until I did something about this stubbly hair that kept coming back.

A few weeks into my no shaving experiment, I put on a pair of tall socks to keep my legs warm. I hated the feeling of the hair between my leg and the sock. I wasn't used to this.

By the way, I told no one what I was doing. You can't expect everyone, even believers, to understand or agree with the things that God calls you to do.

I made it to approximately day 30 without shaving, and I was so eager to shave again. I didn't like the look or the feel of this change. I had been shaving for over twenty years – more years of my life than I hadn't shaved. I felt that I couldn't wait to shave again, but God spoke to me and asked me to go without shaving for 3 full months.

This meant two more months. I didn't want to shave and then have to start the three months all over again, so I agreed to go the additional two months without shaving.

Just when you're ready to stop doing something that you know God put on your heart to do, you may be on the verge of a major breakthrough. I thought that I had done good going 30 days without shaving, but 30 days wasn't long enough for the breakthrough. Getting unbrainwashed from decades of a certain mindset may take longer than 30 days.

Something happened between the second and the third month. I actually began to accept the hair that had been trying to come through for years. I stopped hating the hair that I had

## To Shave or Not to Shave?

continually rejected and immediately gotten rid of for so long. I stopped hating what God had put there. My mind began to adjust to what a woman actually looks like in her natural state. I began to know and accept myself more.

Without knowing it at the time, I was beginning to take back part of my identity. Instead of being in a continual state of self-rejection, I was coming into a place of self-acceptance – accepting the way that God had made me.

I found that the full-grown hairs on my legs were actually very soft. When I had shaved, my legs usually felt prickly and rough because the stubble of the broken, shaven hairs was always trying to come back through. Now, I have full-grown hairs on my legs, and my legs feel softer than when I was shaving.

The same was true for my underarms. At some point, I said, "Oh, hello," to my underarm hair.

I literally had to get reacquainted with parts of me that had been gone for a long time. I learned that I didn't know my own body or my own hair. I had successfully gotten rid of what God continued to bring back for decades. Do you all realize how sad this is? It really is sad. There's so much deception that we accept and never even question. God wants to unbrainwash us.

I believe that first shave as a child was the beginning of part of my identity being stolen. Instead of being carefree and accepting myself the way that God had made me, I became self-conscious. I then hated the sight of what had never bothered me before. I even felt shame and felt that I couldn't wear certain things or participate in normal activities if I hadn't freshly shaved my legs. I had accepted a mindset regarding shaving and had acted on it. Shaving put me on a journey that I stayed on for over twenty years.

Thankfully, by the end of month three of no shaving, the breakthrough had come, and I wasn't eager to shave anymore.

Until I experimented with not shaving, I had no idea how much self-rejection is associated with shaving. After a person accepts a mindset that shaving is necessary or preferred and then begins to shave, every time that hair naturally reappears in these places, consciously or subconsciously, that individual will often think things like, "You don't belong, are not welcome, and I must get rid of you. I will look better without you." This is self-rejection.

Fear of man and conforming to the world are also involved in these mindsets. "What will others say or think if I don't shave?" This is fear of man and fear of rejection. "I must do what everyone else is doing and what they expect from me." This is a prime example of what conforming to the world looks like. I know; I did it for decades.

There's so much self-rejection, shame, and hatred that are attached to shaving. It's a very liberating thing to be able to accept myself in my natural state. It's great when there's nothing about me that needs to be "fixed."

I've actually grown to love the hair that God has given me on my legs and under my arms. It's wonderful and freeing to not need to alter myself. I want everyone to experience this freedom.

Hair on a woman's body was never a supposed "problem" when women stayed more covered. The more that women have uncovered or exposed themselves, the more Satan has attacked their identity.

Every time that women have given in to showing more of themselves, the world and the devil are waiting to tell them what is "wrong" with them and how they can "fix" themselves or make themselves more "attractive" or "presentable." The world will give you a standard that is unnatural that you need to supposedly measure up to. This now angers me.

The things that the world and the devil want us to do to ourselves are actually meant to welcome demonic spirits of insecurity, shame, self-rejection, and lust. The devil wants us to be confused, insecure, and bound.

Once more of one's skin is exposed, the world will also tell you that there's something wrong with your skin and skin color. Once your body shape is more exposed, the world will tell you that there's something wrong with it too. Once your hair is exposed, the world will tell you that it could be better if it were only different, altered, or changed in some way. It's a seemingly never-ending cycle.

People are not content or satisfied after altering or changing one thing. The devil then shows them something else to "fix" or "make better." But the devil cannot make better what God Himself has made.

## To Shave or Not to Shave?

These attacks are not just against us as the created masterpieces that we are. They are also against our Creator. The devil is jealous of the way that God has uniquely and wonderfully designed each person. God has given each of us a unique imprint of Himself.

If we are not ok with any part of how God made us, we are actually not just rejecting ourselves; we are also, in one sense, rejecting the One who made us. It's as though we think that He could've done a better job or should have done a better job.

A person's true identity gets very lost if he or she comes into agreement with these lies that are straight from the pit of hell. I know this very well. I believed these lies for many years.

I have now experienced both sides of this. I shaved for more years than not – approximately 24 years at the time of this writing. For the past 3½ years, I have not shaved a single time.

The devil is strategic. What is it about hair? There's something spiritual about our hair. Hair is strongly connected to a person's identity, which is why it has been under attack.

So much has been taken from us, and we haven't even been aware! But that is changing right now in the earth in the name of Jesus.

Inevitably, when women are affected, men will also be affected, and vice versa. If either loses any part of their identity, the other gender is also affected.

Where were the men when shaving started being promoted as necessary for men or women? Did any of them speak up or even recognize the negative effects that this brought?

Many men have also been brainwashed regarding shaving. They've been told and led to believe that they look unkempt, homeless, or unattractive if they let their mustaches or beards grow out. Where does this thinking come from? It's crazy.

In the past, many jobs and militaries have even forbidden men to have God-given facial hair. This is ridiculous!

The devil is a liar. Beards and mustaches are manly and God-given. Of course, Satan doesn't want men to be manly.

Think about it. Little boys can't grow a beard. Most women can't grow much of one. Beards are a distinguishing mark of manhood.

Think about a male lion's mane. It's awesome, and it sets

them apart as the males. The world, which is strongly being influenced by the devil, has been able to convince many men to get rid of the very thing that is a distinguishing mark of their manhood.

Beards are powerful. To me, a man with a full-grown beard is saying, "This is me, and I don't care what you or anyone else thinks." That is a sign of strength and identity. It's very manly.

More men have been discovering this fact. God has used some men on a television show in the U.S. to help tell the world that it is ok for men to have full-grown beards. Interestingly, these men with full beards are confident and successful. Is this a coincidence?

I've been told that men's razors can wear out quickly, partially due to the texture or coarseness of a man's facial hair. It's interesting that men are typically physically stronger than women, and the hair on men's faces is "tough" in one sense. I wonder how it affects a man when this God-given "toughness" is regularly removed.

Samson had a special strength connected to the hair on his head, which was not to be cut. This strength enabled him to rescue Israel from their enemies, the Philistines. After Samson's hair was cut, he lost his strength, and his enemies were able to defeat him and their people (Judges 13:1–16:21). What strength is lost when men shave or cut the hair on their faces? What enemies are able to defeat them because of this? Who are the men unable to rescue because of this lost strength?

One man that I know has had a beard since I first met him. Recently, he shaved his face before he interviewed for a different job. When I saw him with a shaved face, I was shocked. Although this man was in his thirties, he looked like a little boy. I suppose that this is what the devil wants: men to look and act like boys instead of men.

The natural and the spiritual are connected. "However, the spiritual is not first, but the natural, and afterward the spiritual" (I Corinthians 15:46, NKJV). This states that the natural precedes the spiritual. So, if a person regularly shaves off what God gave him or her in the natural, what is he or she stripping away in the spiritual realm?

Hair is a God-given covering, and there are spiritual consequences when it is removed.

## To Shave or Not to Shave?

In the airport today, I observed a man probably in his thirties with a full-grown mustache and beard. I say full-grown because it was quite long and uneven. Between his mustache and his beard, I almost couldn't see that he had lips. The hair on his head was neatly cut and short. He was dressed nicely and had an attractive wife and two young children.

I couldn't help but notice him repeatedly. He had a confidence that is extremely rare and appealing. He seemed to know who he is, and it really didn't matter what anyone else thought. There was a strength about him.

Another time in the grocery store, I saw two men with long, full beards. I was wearing a headscarf that day that covered all of my hair. As one of the men passed me, he looked into my eyes and nodded respectfully. I could see the mutual understanding and respect that we had for one another. No words had to be spoken. Regardless of who likes it or approves, we both know who we are and are willing to stand out and go against what the culture tries to put on us. I couldn't stop smiling. It was an awesome moment.

One man who has a lot of revelation on hair mentioned something about beards that stuck with me. He said that the devil goes after a man's voice. When a man allows his beard to grow out fully, particularly long enough to cover the man's voice box or Adam's apple on his neck, it provides a type of protection over the man's voice. This makes sense with the natural preceding the spiritual. This also ties into my wearing a head covering. I'm not only honoring the Lord as the head of my life, but I'm also keeping an additional covering on my head, which serves as a protection in the unseen realm from the demonic.

As Christians, we are all priests (I Peter 2:9). Priests were instructed not to shave their heads or trim their beards (Leviticus 21:5-6). Anytime God instructs us to not do something, He is looking out for what is best for us.

I believe that men go through their own liberation when they allow their facial hair to grow out fully. They come into a much greater place of revelation of who they are and find it easier to be their true selves when they get free in this area. Confidence replaces insecurity. I believe that their voices and authority are also restored.

Think about it. How much different would a man look if he went from a completely shaven face to a full mustache and beard? He would look like a different person. Exactly! The devil has people going around looking like someone else as they strip away what God has given them.

It's time for the men to take back their manhood.

This attack has even gone so far as to attack pubic hair. Little boys and little girls don't have pubic hair. This is something that God gives young men and young women as they mature. Yet, the world and the devil have attacked this too. Of course, there is a motivation behind all of these things.

Not only does the devil want us insecure and unprotected, but he also wants to desensitize people to pedophilia. He wants to use pornography and other unnatural images of men and women with little or no pubic hair to desensitize people to pedophilia. The devil doesn't want there to be any distinctions between adults and children. He also doesn't want there to be any distinctions between men and women, but that's a topic for another time.

Although some who get caught in pedophilia and child pornography were themselves first victimized as a child, for many others, I believe they were desensitized in this area through pornography that included images of adults with little or no pubic hair.

Is it any wonder that the devil wants grown men and grown women to look like little boys and little girls by altering and stripping their God-given physical maturity and pubic hair from them? There is a demonic spirit behind these things that attack our identity. And yes, it goes right down to our most intimate parts.

It's so important that people guard their eyes. So many things are meant to steal from God's ways and God's design. Many images that people are looking at are unnatural and are set up against our true identities and against pure, loving relationships.

I even heard that many "women" in the pornography industry are actually men who have had surgeries to make themselves look like women. There is so much deception in the world.

Hair is more significant than we have known. Think about

## To Shave or Not to Shave?

when something isn't right, or there seems to be danger nearby. What happens? The hair on one's arms or the back of their neck often stands up. Hair can alert us to the fact that something isn't right. Do we believe that there is no purpose for the hair that God has put on all of the different parts of our bodies? Do we think that we know better than God?

A friend of mine, who wanted to abstain from sex outside of marriage, once mentioned that she wasn't going to shave her legs before she went on a date with a man. This seemed to help her avoid going further physically with a man than she wanted to go. It seemed to provide some kind of protection against doing anything unholy.

Is this part of why the world wants women uncovered and exposed under their arms and on their legs? It's interesting that these areas are connected to a woman's breasts and her other private area. Is this part of the devil's strategy for women to be more sexually vulnerable and active outside of a marriage covenant?

What are women giving up when they shave their hair? And what are women drawing to themselves when they are shaven and uncovered?

In Jeremiah 7:29, NIV, cutting off one's hair is associated with sorrow after rejection and abandonment. Are spirits of rejection and abandonment welcomed when a person regularly cuts hair off the places that God has put it? Again, the natural precedes the spiritual.

People came into agreement with what the world told them and showed them that a woman and a man should look like. People are still doing this.

There is a mindset, particularly amongst many Caucasians in the United States, that hair isn't acceptable on a woman's legs or under her arms. The thinking seems to be that it is gross or manly for a woman to have hair where God put it.

How much sense does it make that it is supposedly "gross" for a woman to have hair on her legs, yet it's fine to have hair on her arms? Why is it ok for men to have hair under their arms and on their legs but supposedly not ok for women?

It's stupid and unrealistic, and it creates all kinds of self-esteem and self-hatred issues. Many people don't recognize this because they themselves have these issues. It's time for these ridiculous mindsets to come down now in the name of Jesus.

The origination of a thing can tell us a lot about its motives. Guess where the first mention of shaving takes place in the Bible? Egypt. Egypt was known for enslaving the people of God, the Israelites. Genesis 41:14, NKJV, states, "Then Pharaoh sent and called Joseph, and they brought him quickly out of the dungeon; and he shaved, changed his clothing, and came to Pharaoh." A mindset of getting shaven before you present yourself seems to have originated in Egypt. Anything intended to steal from a person's identity has an even deeper origination. These things come from Satan.

I find it interesting that God likes to cover us and to protect us. He did this in the Garden for Adam and Eve. He gives us hair and clothing to cover ourselves. Satan on the other hand likes to uncover and expose us. He wants us to have little or no hair or clothing. Hmm.

Hitler's cohorts in World War II often shaved the heads of the men and women that they took into captivity. Coincidence?

The devil has ill-intentioned reasons that he wants men and women to shave their God-given hair. Hair is strongly connected to each person's identity, which is why Satan attempts to convince the world that it doesn't "look good" and is supposedly "unacceptable" to keep your natural hair.

Frankly, there are more important things than looks. And often times, a person's vision has been tainted by the world, which is influenced by the devil. We need God to purify our eyes, our minds, and our hearts so that we can see things as God does. It's time to take back what the devil has stolen!

Freedom! Can you hear the sound of it? I do. Let freedom ring throughout the earth!

The man who I mentioned earlier with revelation on hair understands that men are less likely to fully use their voices and their authority when they shave their natural, God-given hair from their faces and necks, leaving their throats exposed. The devil wants both men and women exposed and uncovered in the natural realm, which subjects them to more demonic activity in the spiritual realm.

If we are exposed in the natural, what are we being exposed to in the spiritual? What are women's legs being exposed to spiritually? What are men's voices being exposed to spiritually? And the list could go on and on. And what about people's private parts? Jesus, help us.

Please keep the natural coverings that God gives you. They are more significant than we have known. God did not make a mistake in any of these things.

Do you think that God told Eve that she needed to "fix" how He had made her? Do you think that Adam found her unattractive in any way in her natural state? Do you think that hair on a woman's body has halted or hindered God's plans for reproduction in any way?

It is time. It's time to rise up. It's time to take a stand and take back what has been stolen from us. It's time to walk in confidence instead of insecurity. It's time for us to walk in our true identities.

I saw an interesting video that went viral after a dad completely shaved his beard off. His two-year-old son seemed traumatized after the dad removed his beard. The boy wouldn't stop crying when he saw his dad, and he seemed afraid of him. I don't think that he recognized his own father. In order to try to get the two-year-old to stop crying, one of the man's other young sons said to the dad, "Show him the real you." The son called the dad "the real you" referring to when he had a beard.

Listen to the children. Sometimes, they are here to teach us. Their purity enables them to see and speak truth more clearly than many adults.

Seek this out for yourself. Ask God about it. Test this for yourself. God wants all of His creation to walk freely and confidently as He created us to be, not as the world has tried to tell us is "expected" or supposedly "attractive."

Shaving is connected to self-rejection, self-hatred, and shame; being natural (not shaving) is connected to self-acceptance, self-esteem, and confidence.

God, change our vision; change our minds; change our hearts. Help us to see You, ourselves, and others as You do. Help us take back what has been stolen from us.

The natural draws love; the unnatural draws lust. The majority of the things that people are doing to themselves physically are meant to stir up and draw spirits of lust.

Lust is a counterfeit to love. The devil tries to provide a perverted or tainted counterfeit. The devil doesn't want us to have love in our lives. The devil knows that lust will never satisfy or fulfill a person.

God created beauty, desire, and attraction; spirits of lust pervert those things.

A lot of people haven't understood or known what true beauty is. There has been so much blinding and deception. Many people have believed that altered and unnatural images are what are "beautiful." Natural is what is truly beautiful.

Satan hates real, because real is what is powerful. It's time that we get smarter than him.

There's good news. If you're reading or hearing this, it's not too late to change. Samson's hair grew back, and as it did, his strength returned. Samson was then able to conquer more enemies than he had in his entire life before his hair was ever cut (Judges 16:22-30).

Redemption is available. It's not too late to have your strength returned and to conquer your enemies.

Your hair – keep it. Own it. Be you. You're awesome.

What would happen in this world if each person chose to stop shaving and chose to show the world, as the little boy said, the real you?

What change is God asking you to make today?

Next, I would discover something else that had been stolen from me.

# 7

## Rest

When I was in a very busy season of my life in 2018, God said to me, "Rest is a weapon."

I was trying to finish my first book, was working a full-time job, and was leading in a prison ministry. God put on my heart to set aside a whole 24 hours for rest every weekend. This seemed like the worst time to begin doing this. There was so much that needed to be done.

Up to this point, my perception of having a Sabbath wasn't a positive one. As a teenager, I had attended a banquet at a church. The woman who spoke at the event talked about not putting gas in her car and not cooking on Sundays. She talked about making sandwiches on Saturday and putting them in the fridge for Sunday. These were some of the ways that she honored the Sabbath and avoided doing "work." This sounded ridiculous to me. Putting gas in the car doesn't exactly seem like "work" to me. Eating cold sandwiches from the day before also didn't sound like any fun.

I never personally knew anyone who treated one day of the week much different than all the rest. But as I grew in my relationship with God in my adult years, anytime I read in the Scriptures about the Sabbath, I felt a tugging on my heart that I should intentionally set aside some time for rest.

Sometimes, it can seem hard to break old habits and start new ones. Eventually, I started setting aside maybe 3 or 4 hours to do nothing one day each weekend. I would put a reminder in my phone to do this. After a few hours of rest, I would immediately feel more energized.

In March 2018, I heard a message that gave me the breakthrough that I needed. A pastor explained that after being in ministry for many years, he thought that he was losing his mind. He went to simply get a pair of socks from the drawer, and there weren't any there. He couldn't think clearly enough to figure out how to get more socks. His brain couldn't compute to simply wash some that were dirty or go to the store and buy more. Needless to say, he needed a break, so, he went on a sabbatical.

He said that it took him 53 days off work before he started

to feel "normal" again. On the 53$^{rd}$ day, God spoke to him and said, "You were 53 Sabbaths behind." The man replied, "You mean that I owed You 53 Sabbaths?" God replied, "No, you owed you 53 Sabbaths."

When I heard this, I was so stirred to make a change in my life. I always felt that I should honor the Sabbath when I read about it in Scripture, but I never really knew anyone who did this or how to do it. This testimony seemed to break off any more of my delays or excuses.

Planning for the Sabbath is probably the most important step. If I didn't plan for it, it wouldn't have happened. I had to figure out which 24-hour period I could have free from all other responsibilities.

I read that the Israelites were not to leave their homes on the Sabbath (Exodus 16:29). I decided that for me, Sabbath would mean 1) Staying home 2) Rest 3) Leaving my phone off 4) Doing as little as possible around the house 5) Enjoy.

One of the strongest promptings that I had from God was to definitely not go to church on my Sabbath. If I have to get up, get ready at a certain time, and be somewhere at a certain time, that is not rest. Church can also be a primary place where spiritual warfare happens. That is also not rest.

I needed to leave my phone off in order to be free from distractions and anything that could disturb my peace. Satan loves to try to use others to interfere with what God is doing in our lives. Turning off phones and staying off the internet can be important ways to guard one's peace.

At first, I thought, what in the world am I going to do for 24 hours? How would I occupy myself? So, I prepared what I lovingly refer to as a "Sabbath box."

In it, I put things that I could utilize during my Sabbath. These are things that I enjoy, things that wouldn't feel like work in any way. It included good movies, which is one of my favorite things; an adult coloring book with colored pencils; a journal; my Bible; and a couple of other books. I found myself really looking forward to my first true Sabbath of 24 hours.

I decided to clean my apartment in advance so that there wouldn't be anything that needed to be done. I also preplanned my meals. I tried to have premade items that simply needed to be put in the oven.

## Rest

My first Sabbath came. It was a Friday night. I turned my phone off and got my Sabbath box out.

I didn't even know where to start. Sometimes, we don't even know how to rest after never having done it for any length of time.

Subconsciously, my mind seemed to start clearing out all of the cares of the world. There was a wonderful peace that I felt within the first hour.

Something shifted, and I started crying. I sensed that I had been missing out on something in my life for many years, and now, I was taking it back. It was as though Satan had stolen this from me without me even knowing it.

Why wasn't anyone else in my Christian community doing this and talking about it? What could be bad about resting and letting God take care of whatever needs to be taken care of?

Psalm 46:10a, NKJV, says, "Be still, and know that I am God." That's right. He is God; we don't have to be. There's a power in stillness and in rest. He's got this; we don't have to. We can say no to unnecessary pressure.

We can miss out on a lot if we are deceived. I can't even explain how wonderful that first Sabbath was. It was a consecrated time – almost like a date night with the Lord. It wasn't really for His benefit though; it was a gift for me. I wasn't necessarily talking to God a lot. I simply accepted a gift that He wanted me to have.

Honoring the Sabbath isn't something that I have to do; it's something that I get to do. God loves us so much. He wants us to rest and enjoy. Enjoying and resting is exactly what I do on the Sabbath. It's not about rules and what you can and can't do. It truly is a gift, and I'm so thankful that I finally discovered it.

I find that I'm so motivated and refueled for the next week after my Sabbath, especially when I have my Sabbath from Friday evening to Saturday evening. I'm not bound to this time; I've had it many times from Saturday evening to Sunday evening when I've had prison ministry on Saturdays.

God does give us freedom in these things. Although I still have a Sabbath when I change the day, for me personally, I don't usually feel as rested when I begin my Sabbath on any night other than Friday. There's something special about Friday nights.

Recently, God had me join a house church that meets on Friday nights. It was different for me to incorporate this into my Sabbath after not having church as part of my Sabbath for over three years. I believe the fellowship is part of why God wants me there.

It's important to simply obey God in these things. Your Sabbath may look different than mine, and that's ok. Your Sabbath may also look different in different seasons.

One of my Spanish-speaking friends pointed out that the very word "Saturday" in Spanish is "sabado." Sabbath is literally in the name. It's no wonder why this day seems to be the best one for a Sabbath. From the beginning, God knew best when He rested on the seventh day of the week. How did we get so far from this?

Some believe that the concept of a Sabbath was in the Old Testament and is part of rules that we no longer need to follow now that Jesus has come and fulfilled the law. Yet, God Himself rested on the $7^{th}$ day before any of the laws or rules came about. God rested before sin came into the world.

Genesis 2:2-3, NLT, says that God rested or ceased from all His work on the seventh day. Think about the word "cease." It means to stop. Sometimes, we simply need to stop.

Then it says that He blessed the seventh day and declared it holy. It's no wonder why I get more out of my Sabbath when I have it from Friday evening until Saturday evening. The seventh day is declared a holy day. And in Genesis 1, the new day actually starts in the evening. In some parts of the world, businesses are closed on Saturdays.

Do you think that this principle has changed? "Therefore the children of Israel shall keep the Sabbath, to observe the Sabbath throughout their generations as a perpetual covenant" (Exodus 31:16, NKJV).

Did you know that honoring the Sabbath is the $4^{th}$ commandment of the 10 commandments? God put this in the same set of rules that tell us not to murder. That's how important the Sabbath is!

"Remember that you were once slaves in Egypt, but the Lord your God brought you out with his strong hand and powerful arm. That is why the Lord your God has commanded you to rest on the Sabbath day" (Deuteronomy 5:15, NLT). Not resting is a sign of bondage and slavery. Having a Sabbath literally sends a message into the earth that says, "I am free. I am not bound to anything, and I can and do say no to the rest of the world for 24 hours each week." Didn't Jesus pay a high price for our freedom? What are you bound to?

Are you treating the 7th day different than all the rest?

When the man I mentioned earlier didn't choose to rest, it eventually caught up with him. His body and his mind came into a condition that forced him to rest. In Leviticus 25:4, it says that even land needs rest for a whole year every seven years. There is something about rest.

Sometimes, it takes me several hours to decompress from that particular week. Imagine how much decompressing we may need if we are decades' worth of Sabbaths behind.

There is a releasing and letting go that naturally happens during my Sabbath. It's like a weekly deliverance. Also, there is a renewal and a rejuvenation that takes place. Our minds and our bodies were made with a need to rest.

Why do some people feel guilty doing what we were made to do? God Himself rested, and I give you permission to rest.

I've learned that I accomplish more and am more efficient in the next week when I have a Sabbath. I can only imagine the benefits of a weekly Sabbath to one's health, especially to their stress level and blood pressure.

How many ailments would go away if people accepted this gift of weekly rest and ceased from all work for 24 consecutive hours each week?

The Word tells us to "Cast all your cares upon Him, for He cares for you" (I Peter 5:7). Having a weekly Sabbath is one way to let go of your cares and to let God be God.

Rest involves trust. The world will make it ok without you "doing" for 24 hours each week. And yes, people will live without being able to access you for 24 hours. It's a wonderful thing to simply be and not have to do. Just breathe and enjoy.

I heard one person say that we are human beings, not human doings. So, be, and stop doing for at least 24 consecutive hours each week.

I was once invited to an event on a Friday night. The Christian woman looked at me crazily when I responded, "I can't, as that's when I have my Sabbath."

It's sad that the devil has been so successful at stealing God's blessings from us through deception. Many people don't seem to understand the blessing of having a Sabbath. The church hasn't done a very good job of teaching us about a lot of things.

Before we judge anything, why don't we take it before God and ask Him what He thinks? I too have been guilty of thinking that I knew the right answer on something that I really didn't know. Thankfully, God continued to try to get through to me regarding the Sabbath until I finally got it and actually began to rest for a full 24 hours each week.

Traditions can be a terrible thing. Just because we've been doing something a certain way for a long time, that doesn't mean that it's the best way or that it's God's way.

The Scriptures say that we will do what Jesus did and greater (John 14:12). I'm ready to do the greater. It's time to get rid of these mindsets that are not of God and that hinder us from walking in all that God has for us.

Why would resting for 24 hours be bad?

I look forward to my Sabbath. I find myself often wanting it to last longer than 24 hours. That is a true Sabbath – one that you don't want to end.

I hope that everyone will experience the joy and the gift of having a Sabbath. Exodus 16:29, NLT, says that the Sabbath is the Lord's gift to His people. Rather than rejecting this gift, why not receive it? God never gives bad gifts.

It's an amazing thing to simply let go and just be. If you press into this, I can't imagine you ever going back to the way things used to be before having a Sabbath.

What is God speaking to you in this area? What step will you take today?

Rest wasn't the only thing that the church had neglected to teach me about.

# 8
## Getting Rid of the Old

Several years ago, I went through a major emptying season. I had stuff from decades ago that I had been hanging on to. With God's help, I got rid of clothing, dishes, knickknacks, keepsakes, and eventually, furniture. As I let go of those things in the natural, I could literally feel weight leaving me. I wasn't just getting lighter in the natural; I was also getting free spiritually.

Physical things are connected to spiritual things. "However, the spiritual is not first, but the natural, and afterward the spiritual" (I Corinthians 15:46, NKJV).

"Do not remember the former things, nor consider the things of old. Behold, I will do a new thing, now it shall spring forth; shall you not know it? I will even make a road in the wilderness and rivers in the desert" (Isaiah 43:18-19, NKJV). We are to forget the former things. We are not even to think about them, much less hold on to them.

Scripture says that we go "from glory to glory" (II Corinthians 3:18, KJV). We go from glory to glory. Going requires leaving some things and some people behind. We can either stay stuck in the old glory, or we can go into the new season and the new glory that God has for us in this season. Even though I had some great experiences in the past, those were old seasons. God is now doing something new.

Over the past several years, I've completely emptied my life of old furniture, clothing, and other things. I've even cut off communication with certain people from my past.

Why would I want reminders of or connections to the past when God has a much better future for me? Why would I want to stay stuck in the old glory, the old revelation, and the old growth in my life? Why would I want to stay connected through social media or otherwise to some people that God no longer has in my life for a reason? Those things and relationships are now stale and expired.

Food has an expiration date. At some point, food goes bad. Spiritually, things have an expiration date. What has expired in your life?

We outgrow some things and some relationships spiritually.

## Stolen Identity

Think about when you were a child growing in your physical body. As your body grew, you outgrew the clothes that you wore the year before or even a few months before. It's the same spiritually. Physical things keep us spiritually connected to old seasons. What things and what relationships have you outgrown?

I was watching a video of the stages of a caterpillar transforming into a butterfly. You should look this up. In order for the caterpillar to become a butterfly, it has to shed some layers along the way. As the caterpillar grows, the exterior skin does not grow with it, so it has to shed that layer. This happens multiple times before it becomes a butterfly. It has to first get rid of the old before it can receive its wings. We also must shed the old layers and the old things in the natural if we want to fully move forward spiritually into all that God has for us.

Your things don't grow with you, which is why they need to be gotten rid of. Things can weigh you down and even prevent your growth. They can be like a trap.

You may be thinking that your things have monetary value. This may be true, but holding on to those things from the past can cost you much more than the money you already spent. That money is gone. It's finished. What about the better things that God wants to release to you now?

Do you think that your past is better than your future? The reality is that holding on to those things can prevent God from giving us the upgrades that He has waiting. When a person's life is full of the old, there is no room for the new.

When I bought new clothing or a new household item, God led me to get rid of something that I already had. It's like I was exchanging the old for the new. It feels awesome to get rid of things. I literally feel lighter every time I get rid of something.

It felt amazing when I got rid of my last vehicle that I had had for 14 years. It included way too many connections, memories, and people from my past. It felt great to get it out of my life.

When I trusted God enough to first get rid of the old car, God then blessed me with a brand-new car. I got rid of my car before I knew how I would get my next car. Faith was required. Faith paid off. My new car is an amazing upgrade.

What have you been holding on to for too long? What is

## Getting Rid of the Old

God asking you to let go of by faith? What upgrades await you?

Have you ever shopped for something that was difficult to find? I've had this problem with clothing. When God told me to get rid of a skirt that I owned, I hesitated. It had been difficult for me to find this skirt. But God reminded me that as I trust Him and make room for the new in my life, He will replace those things with something even better. Within a week of my getting rid of that skirt, God blessed me with three new, better quality ones! And they weren't even hard to find! Faith works.

Even when I get rid of fairly recent things by taking out the trash or getting rid of expired things in the refrigerator, I feel great and lighter each time.

Jesus told the disciples to travel with only a walking stick (Mark 6:8-9). God wanted to show up and provide for them as they trusted Him enough to leave their old things behind. God wanted to do something new in and through them, and He didn't want them carrying things from their powerless pasts.

I don't like buying used items. God doesn't lead me to buy them either. I don't want anything connected to anyone else's old season. They got rid of those things for a reason. And what is connected in the unseen realm to those items?

Jesus definitely modeled the idea of getting new, pure, unused items. He directed His disciples to get an unridden colt for Him. "As they approached Jerusalem and came to Bethphage and Bethany at the Mount of Olives, Jesus sent two of his disciples, saying to them, 'Go to the village ahead of you, and just as you enter it, you will find a colt tied there, which no one has ever ridden. Untie it and bring it here' " (Mark 11:1-2, NIV).

Jesus' body was also laid in a new tomb. This is no coincidence. "Then he took the body down from the cross and wrapped it in a long sheet of linen cloth and laid it in a new tomb that had been carved out of rock" (Luke 23:53, NLT).

"Therefore, if anyone is in Christ, he is a new creation; old things have passed away; behold, all things have become new" (II Corinthians 5:17, NKJV).

"Then He spoke a parable to them: 'No one puts a piece from a new garment on an old one; otherwise the new makes a tear, and also the piece that was taken out of the new does not match the old. And no one puts new wine into old wineskins; or else the new wine will burst the wineskins and be spilled, and the wineskins will be ruined. But new wine must be put into new wineskins, and both are preserved' " (Luke 5:36-38, NKJV).

The new will not match or fit the old. If things are not changing in your life, even in the natural, it's time to do a spiritual checkup. God doesn't want us stagnant. As God transforms us, the new us doesn't fit into the same old mold. New wine belongs in new wineskins. The new us belongs in new things too.

"Therefore we were buried with Him through baptism into death, that just as Christ was raised from the dead by the glory of the Father, even so we also should walk in newness of life" (Romans 6:4, NKJV). The old things should have been buried. If they haven't been and aren't continually, what new life, new glory, and new things are we missing out on?

I've often found that God will not release the new to us until we by faith get rid of the old. People often want to hold on to the old until they see the new, but that's not how faith works. As we let go of the old, the new can then be released to us.

"However, the spiritual is not first, but the natural, and afterward the spiritual" (I Corinthians 15:46, NKJV). Since the natural precedes the spiritual, what things or people in your life are part of the old season and are holding up the spiritual things that God wants to release to you now in this season?

Ecclesiastes 3:1 states that there is a season and a time for everything. How can you enter into the next season if you're still stuck in the last one? How can you enter into spring if you're still in winter? Even if winter was great, why not move forward into an even better spring?

How is the old stuff in your life preventing you from having room for the new? When did you last get rid of something by faith and trust God to provide an even better replacement?

What is God stirring you to do?

Speaking of new things, there was something else new that God wanted me to know and walk in.

# 9

## Prosperity

Have you heard the term "prosperity gospel" or "prosperity doctrine?" When I have, there's often been a negative connotation associated with these terms.

There's a verse that God has used in my life many times: " 'For I know the plans I have for you,' declares the Lord, 'plans to prosper you and not to harm you, plans to give you hope and a future' " (Jeremiah 29:11, NIV). Although I had memorized this verse, I had mainly focused on the part of Him having good plans for my future. I didn't grasp the word "prosper" until recently. Since it's the Lord's plan to prosper us according to this verse, how is prosperity a debatable "doctrine" or "theology?"

I've been a Christian for many years, yet I didn't have a mindset that God wanted me to prosper. I know lots of Christians that don't seem to be prospering, so maybe I thought that was my fate too. Or maybe I assumed that because Jesus had no place to lay His head, neither would I.

I also grew up hearing about how much everything costs. My mother used coupons and was always trying to get a good bargain. I also got things like socks or other basic needs as "birthday gifts."

We rarely ate out even at a fast food restaurant. If we did, we definitely wouldn't be spending money on a drink. As a child, it seemed that money was limited in our family, and I was very aware of this.

I remember saving up for months to buy my mom a Mother's Day gift. This money came from a small allowance from doing chores and extra work around the yard and the house.

From a young age, I had learned well how to save and not to spend. I also was told when I did get something new that I was to save it for a "special" occasion. So, even when I did get something new like a dress, I was told to basically not enjoy it right now but rather save it for later, for a "special" occasion.

The devil wants to steal our joy in any way that he can. "Don't enjoy what God gives you now." "Be afraid that you'll ruin that new item, so never use or enjoy it." "Don't believe that God will ever give you anything else good. Be afraid of the future." These mindsets are from the devil – that damned devil. Yes, I just said damned. This is a factual statement from the Bible; he is damned to hell (Matthew 25:41 and 23:33, KJV).

It's taken some time, but God has broken a lot off me regarding previous mindsets about life in general and money. I was very good at saving in order to plan for the future, but I was miserable in the meantime.

Saving is often rooted in fear regarding the future. Has God ever not taken care of you? Do you think that He will stop providing for you at some point in the future? This reminds me of when the Israelites were in the desert for many years. God provided them each day with enough manna for food for that day only (Exodus 16). He wanted them to trust Him on a daily basis for their needs and then watch His faithfulness.

God revealed to me that if I hold on to money that He's already given me, I shouldn't expect Him to give me more until I actually use what He's already given me. If the Israelites held any of the manna until the next day, it rotted.

What are you holding on to that is rotten spiritually?

I heard one pastor talk about having a "safety net" of six months' worth of expenses saved. He said that he and his wife kept getting hit with unexpected automobile or home repair expenses when funds were low. He said that once they had a "safety net" in place, those things seemed to stop happening. He felt like Satan was exploiting a weak area. Once they had a "safety net" in place, Satan left them alone.

I do not have a "safety net" of six months' worth of expenses. I have a lifetime of God's favor and provision. The Word says that even the birds do not store food in barns. They do not know where their next meal is coming from, yet God faithfully provides for them (Matthew 6:25-33, NLT).

Do we think that God will do any less for us? He gave us Jesus. He didn't just give us His Son; He gave us all that He had – a complete and total sacrifice. He didn't just give us His first fruit; He gave us His only fruit. God is giving. It's in His nature, and He doesn't change.

In Matthew 25:14-30, there's a parable of a man who leaves for a long trip and entrusts his talents or money to his three servants. When he returns from the trip, two of the workers used what they were given and got a return on their talents. One chose not to use his talent and instead buried or saved it. Verse 25 states that this servant was afraid. The master got very upset with this servant and took what He had given him and gave it to one of the other two workers who actually used what he was given. God told me that this same principle applies now.

I had received some funds after selling my former house in 2016 and had put some of those funds into a savings account. I was holding on to the funds and letting them collect a little bit of interest.

Some months later, I was at a Christian conference. One man of God said these profound words, "You're not going home with a 'give me a discount' mentality." Something broke off me when he said that. Holy Spirit continued to speak to me and told me that I shouldn't expect to be blessed with any more until I use what He's already given me.

God showed me that I needed to use the funds from the home sale and close the savings account. I'm alive now. Life is meant to be lived now, not in the future. And what is being held up from me until I use the stale money from the past?

How many people are sitting on funds and not enjoying life fully because they're living more concerned about the future than they are about the present?

In order to grow, we must act on what God speaks to us. After God told me to get rid of the savings account, He started showing me how to use the funds. He wanted me to enjoy using the funds. He didn't want me to be concerned about the future. "Can any one of you by worrying add a single hour to your life" (Matthew 6:27, NIV)?

I love to travel, and God loves to send me places. I kept hearing and seeing "India," and I knew that was the next place that I was supposed to go. I also love cruising, and I was able to find a cruise that went to India.

I would have to fly from the U.S. to the port in Asia where the cruise set sail from. God strongly put on my heart that I should travel in first class. Paying for first class flights is something that I previously thought was totally crazy. I had actually said in the last two years that I would never pay three times the price of a regular (economy) airline ticket for a first class ticket, since both would get me to the same place in the same amount of time. Never say never.

I'm so glad that God's ways are not my ways (Isaiah 55:8-9). It's easy to say things like that if you've never flown in first class. It's also easy for a person to think that the only thing they've experienced must be the right way or the best way.

When you invite Jesus to come into your heart and are born again into the family of God, you get a new family, a new way, and a new inheritance. My inheritance and family line are now royalty, and so is yours if Jesus is your Savior. The King of Kings is our brother. Prosperity is part of our identity.

Have you ever thought about what royalty looks like? Royalty doesn't worry about money. Royalty doesn't worry about the cost of things. Royalty doesn't fear the future. Royalty doesn't need to use coupons. Royalty doesn't travel in the back of a plane; in fact, they own their own planes. I definitely believe that is in my near future.

I am royalty, period, and so are you, if you're a Christian. Picture a crown on your head, royal garments on your body, and a golden scepter in your hand, as you sit on a throne with Jesus. This is who you are. You are royalty. Say out loud right now: "I am royalty. I am royalty. I am royalty."

Did you actually say it out loud? If not, get to a place where you can and say it. Declare it over yourself. We need to hear the truth in order to be set free. Some of us heard and believed a lot of wrong things for a long time. These things need to be uprooted and cancelled out by us regularly saying, hearing, and believing what God says.

God's plans are to prosper us. Prosperity is our inheritance. Psalm 23:5 says that our cup overflows. Picture a cup overflowing right now. Overflowing means that we have more than enough – more than we need.

Psalm 23:1b, KJV, says, "I shall not want." The NIV translation says, "I lack nothing." Because the Lord is my Shepherd, I will not be in want or lack anything. My cup overflows. These are important truths to speak out loud over yourself until your mind, heart, and soul actually receive and believe them. Speak it until you believe it.

It's taken me years to get to this point. I'm finally getting it, and I want you to get it too.

## Prosperity

I used funds from the savings account to purchase first class airline tickets and the cruise to India. Afterwards, thoughts came to me of how much else I could have done with the funds spent on the first class tickets. Satan tempted me to get a refund on the tickets and fly like I always had in the past: in the back of the plane with no leg room. Satan does not want us to know who we are or to walk in our true identity, which includes fearlessness regarding money.

God had something much better in mind. The Lord kept putting on my heart that this trip, including flying in first class, was part of my upgrade, and I don't just mean in the natural realm.

Everything in the natural is connected to the spiritual. Think about when Jesus was on the Cross. Something was happening in the natural realm and in the spiritual realm. The sky got dark. The veil that separated the rest of the temple from the area of the Holy of Holies that only the high priest was allowed to go into one time per year completely tore. The earth quaked, tombs opened, and many Godly people who had died were raised from the dead (Matthew 27:51-53). Many good things followed Jesus' obedience in the natural. It's the same for us as we obey.

I don't want to miss out on any upgrades that God has for me. I don't want to hold myself back from what God wants to do in my life, so I did not get a refund on the first class tickets and did not downgrade myself to an economy ticket.

Also, I had initially booked the least expensive type of cabin on the ship. God told me to upgrade that too. This was going to use up the rest of my savings. Talk about getting uncomfortable. I liked having that "cushion" or "safety net," but where's the faith in that? Without faith, it is impossible to please God (Hebrews 11:6).

After looking online, I got excited about upgrading my cabin to a suite. I called the travel agent and told him that it was time to upgrade. I knew from the website what the price was and that there was availability. I called while I was in a place of joy, excitement, faith, and readiness to step into my true identity and what God was telling me to do. Guess what happened.

The agent told me that the suite wasn't available for that

price and that it was too expensive. Satan doesn't want us to step into our full identity. He doesn't want us to be joyful, and he will even use other people to try to steal our joy and our upgrades. This man said that what I wanted and saw online wasn't available, and he tried to make me feel like what I was requesting was out of my reach.

I hung up from that call and chose to not accept that answer. Something didn't seem right. I knew that I was doing what God had told me to do. I chose to not let this man or the devil steal my upgrade.

I proceeded to call a second time. I intentionally got a different agent to help me, and guess what happened. Voila, I got my suite cabin! And I got it booked for the exact price that I saw online that the original agent seemed to be unable to help me with.

I then called the original agent and told him that I needed to cancel my original booking with him. I told him that another agent was able to book me the suite that I tried to get him to help me with.

Don't allow anyone or anything to stop what God is wanting to do in your life. If one way doesn't work, go to the next way. There is always a way. Don't allow Satan to stop you if the first answer seems like a no or a blockage. Press through into your breakthrough.

I am on the cruise in that suite now. I'm in the middle of the Arabian Sea on a huge ship. I'm currently listening to the sound of the waves as I sit on my private balcony and type this.

So far, I've had the most amazing couple of days on this trip. I could have easily missed all of this though if I had chosen to keep what I already had: funds in the bank. It would have been easy to not use up that savings account. Honestly, it felt difficult to make the choice to spend thousands of dollars on airline tickets to go overseas first class.

But, I definitely have no regrets. Being called by name and escorted to my spacious seat, being catered to before the plane took off and throughout the flight, and having a bed to sleep in during the flight were just a few of the things that I got to enjoy while flying first class.

If I hadn't listened to the Lord and chosen to walk in these upgrades, I would have much to regret. God wants us to think bigger and to live in much better things. Sometimes, we hold ourselves back because of fear or what seems to be an obstacle. "For God has not given us a spirit of fear, but of power and of love and of a sound mind" (II Timothy 1:7, NKJV).

On the ship, I have more space in this suite than I would've had in the original cabin that I had booked. I also have a private balcony and had fresh flowers waiting for me in my suite. I also get to dine in a separate dining room that is better, smaller, and exclusive to suite guests.

I've received better treatment and better food in the separate dining room. They call me by name and are eager to make sure that I am happy and enjoy myself. They have multiple people available to make sure that this happens. I could tell that they put their best employees in this dining room. The food is definitely higher quality also.

Because Jesus' Spirit lives inside of us, we deserve high quality and should be walking in the best things available. Abraham was wealthy and stood out amongst the unbelievers. We should too. I'm beginning to really understand this as I walk in the things that God leads me to walk in. As we treat ourselves well, we are treating Jesus well, as His Spirit lives inside of us.

I can't imagine not having a balcony on any future cruises. Being able to stay in my pajamas, sit on the balcony, do nothing, and listen to the sound of the waves are such blessings. The first night on the ship, I realized that I could leave my balcony door open and go to sleep with the sound of the waves in the background, so that's what I did. It's heavenly. I love being out in the sea with no land or anything else in sight. It's so peaceful. It's refreshing for the mind, spirit, soul, and body.

I feel like getting up and dancing right now because this journey and life are so amazing. God wants us to enjoy this life. Jesus came so that we might have life and have it more abundantly (John 10:10, NKJV). He desires that we live in abundance. He came for that reason! He wants us to have again all that Adam and Eve first had in the garden when everything was so wonderful.

I'm currently enjoying the very suite that the original agent didn't seem to want or know how to book for me. Satan did not win. Ha Ha.

## Stolen Identity

I'm in amazement. This journey is so wonderful. This is not pride; it's identity. It's destiny.

There is a time for humility, but this is about identity. Too many Christians haven't known who they are in Christ, but this is changing.

It's ok to know that you are important. You are a son of God or a daughter of God. You have purpose. You are here to do great things. You are important, and it's ok to be treated that way.

Christians need to come up into who God says that they are, not who their biological families or others think they should be. We need to walk in what God has for us.

Prosperity is not a doctrine; it's a straight word from God. "If they obey and serve Him, they shall spend their days in prosperity, and their years in pleasures" (Job 36:11, NKJV). There is nothing vague or difficult to understand about what God says about this. There are many Scriptures that talk about God's people who walk in His ways prospering.

I'm so thankful that I'm living my life now and not waiting to live it later. I'm one of the younger people on this ship, particularly amongst the suite guests. I'm also unique in that I am traveling solo. Not having someone to travel with you is not a good reason to not live your life now.

Royalty is who we are. We don't need to apologize for it or act like it's a once in a lifetime situation when we do these things. We are here to prosper and multiply.

This new mindset did not start with a first class ticket. Months before this, God told me to start putting premium gasoline in my car. This is the best quality and the highest cost gasoline available. We are premium. We deserve the best and should walk in the best. Our vehicles should run on the best too. Jesus paid way too high of a price for us to walk in anything less.

God has also had me shopping at high-end grocery stores, which I love because they have better quality items. God wants the best for us. Do we want the best for us? Do we believe that we are worth it? God thinks so, so He sent us Jesus.

There has been a process that has taken place as I've chosen to walk in obedience and not shop for the cheapest things available, whether that be gasoline, groceries, or other things. These seemingly small things are actually big because they affect our mindset regarding money and what we deserve. I don't know that I could have bought the first class ticket before I made these other changes. God is still working on me in this area.

I used to always check my receipts to make sure that everything was exactly right. What if something is a dollar or two off? Is it that big of a deal? Is it worth my time and my peace? I am rich. I am royalty. Do I need to concern myself with those things that used to keep me bound?

That cruise to India was over 2 years ago. I didn't go broke after using up the funds in the savings account. In fact, I paid off the interest-free loan on my car early. I've also gone on three cruises, a trip to Uganda and South Africa, and a trip to Mexico since then. Trusting God pays off. Not fearing the future pays off. The good times in my life haven't come to an end after using those funds. Using those funds has enabled God to release even more to me.

What funds are you holding on to?

Who are you? Whose are you? Do you believe that you are royalty? Do you act like it? I call you up into your God-given identity as royalty.

What step is God asking you to take today?

Are you prospering? Do you believe God's words that He desires to prosper you and to fill your cup to overflowing?

Are you fully enjoying your life? If not, why not? What change does God want you to make today?

Prosperity wasn't the last thing that would greatly impact my identity and destiny.

# 10

# Prophecy

Have you been around prophecy? For many years as a Christian, I wasn't exposed to this gift. Yet, over the years, it has played a major role in my identity and destiny.

Although prophecy was never taught or openly practiced at the church that I grew up in, I did have one very prophetic thing happen to me as a young teenager. The pastor of the church gave me two books from his personal library. The books were about how to write a book. I didn't feel that I was a writer at the time, yet, in my adult years, God confirmed this call and gift in my life.

Prophecy can be released without words. That pastor didn't use any words when he handed me those books, yet this was prophetic. God had given him a download, which he then acted on. That was prophecy. He is a messenger of God. Anyone can be used in this capacity.

Many years later, I was in a church service when I was in my early 30's. There was a woman in front that I had never met before. She had started singing a song, but then, she paused, looked directly at me, and said, "You need to write. People need to know what you've been through." That was probably four years before my first book came out. God used her to water a seed that was already in me about writing. If it weren't for prophecy, I don't know that I would've come into my true identity and destiny and be writing this book now.

I knew that I was supposed to write a book, but I struggled with what to put in it and how to start the process. In 2017, a man of God facilitated a writer's conference. He said that this wasn't his idea, but rather it was something that God had put on his heart to do.

God prompted me to attend that conference, so I did. I experienced a major breakthrough when I was there. Something shifted. For me, the most important things that happened at this conference were that they laid hands on us, and they released impartation to us. At least two of the speakers there had already written and published books and are already walking in their gifts and callings. They have an ability to help us breakthrough into what they have already broken through. II Timothy 1:6, NKJV, says, "Therefore I remind you to stir up the gift of God which is in you through the laying on of my hands." The laying on of hands is powerful for many things.

After the conference, I no longer felt helpless regarding how to start the process of writing a book. I literally went back to my hotel room the night the conference ended and began writing a plan regarding how and when I would complete my first book.

This man heard from God and acted on the message that he had received. That prophetic word, along with the others, contributed to the eventual release of my first book: *I Found God Outside of Church*. That first book coming out was truly a miracle.

Prophecy is so important and truly affects our identity and our destiny. And our destiny is affecting others. If you are not doing what you're here to do, who is negatively being impacted? Who is waiting on you? Prophecy should not be underestimated.

I've also been in church services, conferences, or some other gathering of believers where someone has come to me and shared things that they heard God saying to them about my life. I love when this happens. It's usually been encouraging. I love to hear God's thoughts about me and my life through other people. Destiny and prophecy are closely connected.

Think about Jesus' life. Many things about His life were prophesied long before they happened. It's the same for us as God's children.

God has also spoken things to me to share with someone else. Sometimes, it has seemed like something general and hasn't necessarily made sense to me. But, I've had people come to me later, and the words made perfect sense to them and pertained directly to what they were seeking God about.

One time, God told me that a man would have a change on his job in three months. I wrote this down and gave it to him. Three months later, the man lost his job. The wife later told me that the note that I had given them with that prophetic word encouraged them to know that God had them and knew this was coming. In time, the man got a different job, which led to a promotion that was better than the job he previously had.

I'm usually not asking God for a prophetic word for someone when the prophetic word has come. I'm usually just spending time with the Lord. As I do, He speaks to me, and sometimes when He speaks, it's about or for someone else. We are God's trusted friends.

Have you been prophesied to? Are you intentional about getting connected with believers who operate in prophecy?

Have you prophesied to anyone? Do you desire to? God is looking for vessels who are willing to be used by Him. We are here to help bring others into their God-given destiny.

Are you in a community where prophecy is active? According to Revelation 19:10b, NKJV, the testimony of Jesus is the spirit of prophecy. So, if you're not around prophecy, then you are not around the true testimony of Jesus Christ. There's so much more to Jesus than we know. His depths are deeper than the oceans. Jesus wants us to know why we're here and to then do those things that we're called and gifted to do. He didn't die on the Cross for no reason.

I heard about a group of prophetic people that are connected with a local police department. These men and women of God have helped the police locate missing persons through the gift of prophecy. How awesome is that!

God wants to use His people to magnify His Son Jesus in the earth. Jesus is real. He is the Savior of the world. His sacrifice on the Cross enables us to have eternal life. His Spirit inside of us enables us to know and release things that we otherwise could not know. Let's make ourselves available to magnify and reveal Jesus to the world!

Are you in a church where prophecy operates? If not, your destiny is negatively being affected. Is God leading you to make a change?

What is God speaking to you now? Is He giving you a word for someone? If so, write it down and give it to them. Be the blessing that God created you to be, and don't be afraid of prophecy. It's Jesus manifesting in the earth.

Prophecy hasn't been the only thing that has helped me breakthrough into my destiny.

# 11
## There's Something About Water

Have you ever noticed how many people flock to a beach for their vacation or holiday? What is it about the ocean that draws so many people there for rest and relaxation?

Have you ever wondered why much more of the earth is covered with water rather than with land?

I visited the beach at Tybee Island, Georgia, USA, for the first time in 2011. My friend that was with me squealed with joy and literally ran into the water. She said to me, "It's food for the soul." That stuck with me. She's right.

It's June 2019, and I'm currently out in the middle of the Atlantic Ocean on a large ocean liner. One man on this ship has traveled this particular route from Southampton, England, to Brooklyn, New York, USA, several times. He said that being on the water is "therapeutic."

I love being out on the ocean. When I'm on top of the water on a ship and can't see land or people, it's one of the greatest feelings I've ever felt. There's a peace here that's difficult to explain. I suppose that this is part of why I'm now on my seventh cruise.

I was thinking last night that I could see myself doing one of these transatlantic crossings a few times a year. Part of the appeal to me of this particular voyage is that we are at sea for the entire week of the journey. The only days in port are when we departed and when we arrive at our destination on the last day.

Although I've thoroughly enjoyed many ports that I've been to on previous cruises, sea days tend to be my favorite. There are no responsibilities. There's nowhere to be at any particular time. It's easy to not know what day it is or what time it is. It's like living in a timeless, carefree world. Great food and great housekeeping are included. I get to meet people from all over the world. And most importantly, I have a private balcony so that I can easily access the sound of the ocean waves at any moment.

I've gone to sleep with the sound of the ocean in the background several times. Currently, I get to write as I listen to the ocean waves and worship music simultaneously. For me, this is the ultimate kind of relaxation. There's no place like this. I feel that I could easily stay on this ship for the next month and be quite content. The continual sound and movement of the ocean is so invaluable.

What is it about the ocean that causes this profound peace, tranquility, relaxation, recharge, therapy, and "food for the soul?" If we go back to creation, we will find something pretty incredible. The first time that Holy Spirit is ever mentioned is with water. In the second verse of the entire Bible, before people are ever mentioned, water is mentioned. It says that "the Spirit of God was hovering over the surface of the waters" (Genesis 1:2, NLT).

Whether or not people realize it, when we go to the ocean or near water in general, we're connecting with our roots and with our Creator. This is why people reap such wonderful benefits there. People spend large amounts of money and sometimes use all of their vacation or holiday time to reap the benefits of what they find there.

When I first moved to Savannah, Georgia, in 2011, I found myself at the beach a lot. I had profound experiences with God there, which I discuss in detail in my first book.

Later, the Lord showed me why I went to the beach so much in those first few years. There's healing near water, and I needed a lot of healing. In the Psalms, it says that God leads us beside still waters and restores our souls there (Psalm 23:2-3, NKJV). For some reason, these two phrases were split into two verses, but they belong together. It's near water that our souls are often restored.

Whether or not people understand it, they head to the beach to have their souls restored. It's actually God who leads us there for that refreshment and restoration.

The unique sights and sounds that naturally occur near water are things that we cannot make or do for ourselves. Water is a gift. Isn't it interesting that we can't make water? We need our Creator for our existence in so many ways.

We need the water that God provides to get clean both physically and spiritually. For decades, I've been enjoying long showers. My mind and emotions get refreshed through the showers. Remember that the physical or natural precedes the spiritual (I Corinthians 15:46).

## There's Something About Water

Have you ever had a time when you were unable to shower or fully bathe for more than a day or two? How did that affect you mentally? How did it feel once you finally were able to immerse yourself in water again? Water or the lack of it affects us mentally and spiritually.

Although I was baptized as a child, my true salvation and new birth happened later. For many years, I had in my mind that I had already been baptized and that I didn't need to do it again. I had a mindset that a person should only be baptized once.

In 2016, God prompted me to go to Israel. I was 35 years old. I knew that it would be great to walk where Jesus had walked. The ministry that I went with offered an opportunity to be baptized in the Jordan River, where John baptized Jesus. God told me that getting baptized was the primary thing that He wanted me to do during the trip.

There's often a battle surrounding the very things that will have a great impact upon our lives spiritually. The Lord said to me that I should be dipped in the water three times. I didn't question why. I just knew that I needed to be dipped three times.

During the trip, the lead minister who would be doing the baptisms mentioned that the early Christians were dipped three times. He then said that we should not ask to be dipped three times. I think that this was for the sake of time and the number of people that would be getting baptized. Nonetheless, that is the very thing that God put on my heart to do. What do I do now?

I started scoping out the other men on the tour to see if there was a Godly man that I would feel comfortable asking to dip me three times. I had to resist thoughts that tried to trouble me regarding how this was going to happen. I knew that one way or the other, I would be dipped three times even if I had to do it myself.

I fought the questions, doubts, and insecurities that tried to come to my mind leading up to the baptism. Thankfully, I was already free from wearing makeup and being super insecure about the way that I looked, so that was one less thing that could try to bother me regarding this full submersion in water.

The day for the baptism finally arrived, and I still had no idea how I was going to be dipped three times. I chose to trust God with it.

There was a limited amount of time for the baptisms to take place at this location at the Jordan River, and we had a large group of people to be baptized. These baptisms were not like most church experiences I've seen where the individual or the pastor might share his or her name and a brief summary of why he or she is getting baptized. Instead, one person went forward and got dipped; then, it was on to the next person. Even though it was fast, it was still profound because you're in Israel and in the Jordan River.

I was in line with a bunch of other people. As I got into the water, it was shockingly cold. It felt like I had just stepped into the Arctic. It was November. The air temperature outside was great; it was probably in the 70's (Fahrenheit). I have no idea what the water temperature was though.

I tried to ignore the freezing water and continued to move forward as the line moved. As I approached the two ministers that were doing the baptisms, I held my hand up with three fingers in the air. I quickly said, "God told me to be dipped three times." The lead minister said, "Ok," and before I could think, I was submerged in the water.

They baptized me so quickly that there wasn't time to think about anything, which was probably good. These men were expert baptizers. After dipping me once, they kept my body submerged and in a horizontal position and then barely brought my head up out of the water and right back down again in three swift motions. It was all over in probably less than twenty seconds.

Did you know that your breakthrough could happen in 20 seconds if you're obedient to what God asks you to do?

I moved forward and over to the side to get out of the way of anyone else. I stood there with my eyes closed and lifted my hands. I waited to hear from God or to feel something. I knew that what had just happened was important. What now? Would He tell me something regarding it?

I waited for a few minutes without hearing anything, so I went back inside to the changing area. We had been given white baptismal robes to wear over whatever else we chose to be baptized in. I went into a restroom stall and began changing back into dry clothes. This was probably five or ten minutes after the baptism.

Suddenly, I started weeping – almost uncontrollably. I wasn't even sure why I was crying. Something had happened in that water. It had taken a few minutes for me to comprehend or feel it. First the natural, then the spiritual.

I still can't fully explain the experience except that it was profound and life-changing. I now know that baptism is not simply symbolic of a new birth. Something happens to us spiritually through the water. There's something about full submersion. There's also something about being dipped three times.

I've heard many things that the three times could represent, but I haven't received full revelation on it yet. Some said that it could represent Father, Son, and Holy Spirit. That sounds nice, but it doesn't resonate in my spirit. Another said that it represents death, burial, and resurrection. Again, that sounds great, but I don't sense that that is it either.

Water has more spiritual significance than many have realized. After my experience, I want to be baptized again, unless God specifically tells me not to. It was so great. Why not get blessed multiple times in this way?

I talked to others who also were under a lot of spiritual warfare surrounding their baptisms. The devil definitely does not want you to be baptized. One man on the trip had full intentions of getting baptized, but for some reason, at the last minute, he changed his mind. He spoke to me about it later and said that it would probably always be one of his greatest regrets.

After I got back to the U.S., I talked to a couple who had been to Israel. The husband stated that he had hurt his toe prior to the day of the baptism, and that was his reason for not getting baptized there.

Make up your mind in this area, and don't let anyone or anything stop you. Also, get spiritually armored up, as there is a spiritual battle surrounding baptism. Know that the devil will try to influence you to miss your blessing and breakthrough. He wants to steal that from you; don't let him.

I went many years without this experience and

breakthrough. I've known many women who aren't comfortable with getting their hair wet and things like that in a group setting. Insecurity from the devil keeps them from experiencing that level of vulnerability. That was me for a long time. I praise God that He has freed me. If you're struggling with any of that, simply ask God to help you, and He will.

We also need to drink water to live physically in our bodies. We literally cannot live or function well without water on multiple levels. Water is both physical and spiritual.

Water also invites the fire of God. Sometimes, spiritual laws don't make sense with natural laws. The prophet Elijah once poured water over the wood on an altar in a public display over the false prophets of Baal. He did this to demonstrate who the true God is. Barrels and barrels of water were poured in a trench over and around the animal sacrifice. As Elijah acted in obedience to God and called upon the Lord to consume the sacrifice with fire, the fire of God came down and consumed the sacrifice and the water (1 Kings 18:16-40). There are times when God wants us to use water in the natural in order to bring forth His fire to burn up anything that needs to be burned up.

Recently, my friend and I had the privilege of telling a 9-year-old girl about Jesus. After we told her about Him, I asked her if she wanted to pray and ask Jesus to come into her heart. She did, so we prayed together. After we prayed, she asked me about "holy water." I wasn't sure what she was referring to. She then talked about having her own money that she could buy some anointing oil with. I told her that I had a bottle right there and gave it to her. I didn't think too much more about it until I heard a report a couple weeks later.

My friend relayed that the 9-year-old had been a very fearful child. She had been sleeping in the parents' room her whole life. She also was too afraid to go to friend's houses and things like that. After asking Jesus into her heart, she went home, ran some bath water, and poured a large portion of the anointing oil in the water. She then bathed in the water.

Not too long after that, she asked her mom if she could start staying home by herself. She also wanted to go to friend's houses. The mom was shocked. She asked her daughter what was going on. The child replied, "Jesus healed me."

Isn't that precious? God showed her what she needed to do

to get free, and she did it. Interestingly, it involved water.

In the summer of 2019, I had an opportunity to be baptized again. There was a Christian ministry that traveled around and facilitated baptisms for God's people. Many talked about the fire of God being connected to the baptisms. God put on my heart to be baptized again.

My desire was to be baptized with the fire of God, even though I was being submersed in water. This time, I got dipped only once. I didn't feel anything, yet I'm confident that as I acted in obedience, God accomplished what He wanted to accomplish in me.

When were you last near water for any length of time? What restoration does your soul need? Is it time for you to book a trip? Is it time for you to move closer to water?

I've learned that I'm not the only one who has had profound experiences with God near water. One woman who read my first book stated that she also has had similar experiences with God at the beach. Others have told me the same thing. In Biblical times, the prophet Daniel had visions from God and angelic encounters near water (Daniel 10:4-8). What experiences have you had with God near water?

Water! Go out and have some! Get in some! Visit some!

What is God speaking to you about water today?

Have you been baptized since your new life with Jesus began? If not, why not ask someone about getting this done? If you have been baptized, is God prompting you to publicly receive another blessing in this area?

What else is God asking you to do with water right now? Will you say yes to your breakthrough? Water!

Water wasn't the last thing that God would use to bring me into my true identity and destiny.

# 12

## Does What We Wear Matter?

What does your clothing say about you? Since the natural precedes the spiritual (I Corinthians 15:46, NKJV), what is your clothing preceding spiritually? How is our clothing affecting us and others around us?

As God renewed my mind, I began to realize that I had chosen most of my clothes for the way that I thought they looked on me. What others thought of me seemed to matter more to me than my own comfort.

How had I never noticed the difference between unnatural material like polyester and natural material like cotton? How had I worn certain things every day for years without knowing that there were far better options? Why had I never thought or cared about my own comfort?

Pleasing others with the way that I looked externally helped mask what was going on internally (feeling bad about myself, etc.) Satan wanted to keep me insecure.

But as God's love for me was revealed, I began to love myself more. The more time that I spent with the Lord, the more He transformed me and renewed my mind with His thoughts over those of the world.

God is such an amazing transformer. The more I walked with the Lord and got free, the more secure I became. I began to see myself and my natural beauty more the way that God sees me. I began to understand the way that He intended and created me to look, which is far different than what the world promotes.

Now, I have no need to try to make myself look pretty when God already made me beautiful. I no longer use or desire to use artificial things in the world to make myself look different or supposedly "better." The artificial things are facilitated by Satan and are meant to steal one's confidence and their ability to walk in their true identity.

I also no longer want to draw attention to my figure or the exterior through my clothing. I now know that what I have on the inside is so much more important and valuable than this body that God has given me. What's on the inside will not fade away.

As I've gotten freer, I want to cover myself more and more – not because I'm ashamed of my body but because I know who I am, and I know my worth. When I didn't know who I was, all I seemed to know how to do was to attract people to me through my exterior.

How many women do you see keeping their bodies and body shapes covered? If what is true for me is true for other women, how many women actually know their worth and know who they are?

If you're not yet married, is your body or the exterior the primary thing that you want someone to like about you? What kind of foundation is that? What will happen if the exterior changes? Will someone else's exterior be more appealing later?

Does anyone besides a person's spouse need to know any details about his or her body?

To the men, is it helpful for you in your thought life or in your marriage to see images of other women's figures?

I now want people to be drawn to the Spirit of the living God inside of me, so I try to dress in a way that avoids anything else being a distraction. I am no longer my own. I've been bought with the precious blood of Christ, and I'm called to glorify God with this body that He's given me (I Corinthians 6:19-20). How many people are glorifying God with their bodies, particularly by the way that they dress?

Most men wouldn't do half of the things that women do to make themselves look supposedly "better." Makeup and uncomfortable shoes are just two examples. How many times have you seen women take their shoes off because they are too uncomfortable to wear for very long? This is especially true for high-heeled shoes. This is a problem. And what about uncomfortable clothing?

Many things that we've been trained to think look "good" are actually meant to draw lust. A spirit of lust will never allow a person to be satisfied. A person's natural, God-given beauty is more than enough for procreation to continue as God designed with one's spouse.

Bit by bit, I threw away my previous clothes and replaced them with more comfortable and modest ones that were made from 100% cotton. After wearing cotton on a regular basis, it became hard to put on anything less than 100% cotton. Cotton feels wonderful up against the skin compared to unnatural fabrics. My clothing is now less fitted and covers more too.

It's like I graduated in my thinking. First, I realized that cotton feels better on my skin. Then, I started caring more about how something feels rather than how it might look. I started living my life more for me rather than for what others might think. That is freedom. Then, I started wanting to cover my body more. As I became more focused on my insides, I wanted others to focus on that too.

My joy has increased as I've discovered who I am and have walked and lived accordingly, even by changing my clothes.

Although cotton is good, God led me to something even better: linen! I heard a man talking positively about linen and realized that I always felt great when I wore my 100% linen skirt. I looked up information on linen and found some people testifying that they were healed in their bodies through wearing linen clothes and sleeping on linen pillowcases.

God put on my heart to start buying 100% linen clothing, so I did. I also bought linen sheets. Initially, I didn't like the linen sheets as much as my cotton ones. I was used to the softness of the cotton sheets. Sometimes, linen has to be broken in. Linen softens with more wear and more washes.

Linen has grown on me. I discovered that I felt better when I wore 100% linen clothing.

I thought that finding 100% cotton clothing was difficult in the U.S. Try finding 100% linen clothing, particularly if it's not the spring or summer season. I've learned that there are currently far fewer clothes made from natural fabrics in the stores than there are made from unnatural, uncomfortable materials. I've had much better success finding 100% linen clothing online rather than in the stores.

I discovered that linen wasn't easy to find and was often more expensive than other materials. This confirmed that linen was good for me. The world doesn't often promote the things that are best for us.

Linen is in Scripture a lot. Here are some of the truths that stood out to me.

Jesus was wrapped in linen when He was entombed (Mark 15:46, NLT). Is this coincidental?

Linen is also in the same category as gold, silver, and

bronze (Exodus 25:2-4, NLT). Since linen is mentioned with the best, why wouldn't we want to wear the best?

In Proverbs 31:21-22, NLT, the virtuous and fearless woman wore linen.

Linen is also associated with royalty, richness, honor, and luxury (Luke 16:19 and Genesis 41:42-43, NLT). We as sons and daughters of God are part of a royal family. Do you feel and act like royalty? How is your clothing affecting the way that you feel and act?

If we wear unnatural fabrics in our clothing, do we see ourselves in more unnatural ways? Do we also live in less natural, God-designed ways? Are others also drawn to unnatural things about us? Satan tries to be slick. Again, the natural precedes the spiritual, so how is unnatural clothing affecting people?

In the wedding supper of the Lamb in Revelation 19:6-8, NLT, pure white linen represents the good deeds of God's holy people. This says that our clothing represents something. What is your clothing representing?

Linen is also a sign of being set apart for God (Exodus 28:3-5, NLT).

Wearing linen is also associated with serving the Lord and hearing from God (1 Samuel 2:18, 3:1-4, NLT). The Lord instructed the prophet Jeremiah to wear linen (Jeremiah 13:1, NLT). Visions and prophecies that were given to other prophets also included linen (Ezekiel 40:1-3, Daniel 10:4-7 and 12:5-7, NLT). Will we hear from God more often and with more clarity if we wear linen?

According to Ezekiel 44:17-18, Exodus 28:39-43, and Leviticus 6:10, NLT, linen is to be worn when doing priestly duties. We as believers are priests (1 Peter 2:9, NLT). What are we wearing as we do priestly duties? Are we even doing priestly duties? How is our clothing affecting us?

Linen is also associated with music, worship, and ushering in God's thick presence. "Wearing a linen ephod, David was dancing before the Lord with all his might" (2 Samuel 6:14, NIV). "And the Levites who were musicians – Asaph, Heman, Jeduthun, and all their sons and brothers – were dressed in fine linen robes and stood at the east side of the altar playing cymbals, lyres, and harps. They were joined by 120 priests who were playing trumpets. The trumpeters and singers performed together in unison to praise and give thanks to the Lord. Accompanied by trumpets, cymbals, and other instruments, they raised their voices and praised the Lord with these words: 'He is good! His faithful love endures forever!' At that moment a thick cloud filled the Temple of the Lord. The priests could not continue their service because of the cloud, for the glorious presence of the Lord filled the Temple of God" (2 Chronicles 5:12-14, NLT). Why not wear linen now as you usher in the thick presence of God? The physical and the spiritual are connected.

Angels in heaven wear white linen (Revelation 15:5-6, NLT). Why not have some heaven on earth and wear linen now?

I've also learned that linen is very breathable and less confining. God does not want our destinies or our identities confined.

God also wants us to be set apart from the world. Clothing either sets us apart or has us blending in with the world. Are you set apart, or are you blending in?

We are a peculiar people (I Peter 2:9, KJV). We are also not to be conformed to this world (Romans 12:2).

As we walk with God, He renews our minds. Our thinking, our behavior, our appearance, and even our clothing changes.

I'm transforming my wardrobe yet again, and it's awesome. Being surrounded in my living room by so many new, linen clothing items has brought me incredible joy. It's difficult to explain. Some things have to be experienced. Most of us enjoy getting new things, but this is so much more than that feeling of getting something new. Linen literally brought me joy! It's not explainable; it just is. Living in my true identity brings me great joy!

Many things in the natural are affecting us more than we have known. I'm here to expose the truth. I want to help you discover who God created you to be and help you walk in your true identity. That is where true fulfillment and joy come from – knowing why God created you and then walking in those divine purposes.

Why wait to wear what royalty, priests, and virtuous people wear? Aren't we all of those things now through the blood of Jesus? Would we know our identity better if we put on the material mentioned throughout the Scriptures as best? Satan wants to use clothing to negatively affect our understanding of our identity and to keep us from fully walking in our God-given destiny.

Jesus paid a very high price for us to be fully free. He doesn't want us walking around partially blind, only partially free. He wants us to see ourselves clearly and to walk and move confidently in this world. Your clothing is affecting you. The question is: how is it affecting you?

Linen is more expensive for a reason. It's amazing. Sometimes, you really do get what you pay for.

Linen clothing helps me walk more in my God-given callings and destiny. Others also treat me more as royalty and honor me more since I began wearing linen on a regular basis. I want you to experience the same.

How much of your clothing is made from unnatural materials? What is your clothing speaking to others and to yourself? What change is God asking you to make today?

God not only changed my thinking about what I put on my body, but He also changed my thinking about what I put into my body.

# 13
## First Fasting Experiences

In 2017, I attended a writing conference near Orlando, Florida. I had fasted during the conference and really looked forward to going to one of my favorite restaurants afterward.

When the conference ended, I was really motivated and excited about writing. God prompted me to begin writing that very evening. This meant that I would need to forego my favorite restaurant and instead get something quick through a drive-through in order to get back to my hotel room and begin writing. It was not an easy decision for me to give up my favorite restaurant.

The Lord said to me, "If you don't start writing now, after getting so fired up, when will you?" I knew what I had to do. I made the choice to forego my favorite restaurant. I ate fast food in my hotel room and then spent the rest of the evening writing.

Did you know that food can get in the way of your calling?

Destiny requires sacrifice; sometimes, that sacrifice is food. It's no coincidence that Jesus fasted for 40 days prior to His ministry with the disciples of healing the sick and casting out demons.

Shortly after that writing conference ended, God led me to fast every other day for 40 days while I worked on my first book. I didn't understand at the time that the fast was enabling me to press into my destiny. I needed a lot of breakthrough in order to have courage and wisdom regarding the release of my first book, which includes a lot of personal testimony. It's not always easy to share with the world the most painful seasons of my life, yet fasting gave me strength and focus.

I also fasted at other times throughout the process of working on that first book. If I hadn't, I never would have finished. And if my first book had never come out, this one wouldn't have either. I wonder what we're not accomplishing if we're not fasting.

The power of fasting should never be underestimated. How was I in church for years yet never heard testimonies on this topic? Are Christians fasting regularly?

Jesus told His disciples that some things can only be

accomplished through prayer and fasting (Matthew 17:21, NKJV). This truth hasn't changed.

Why are some Christians in as bad of shape physically and financially as some nonbelievers? Why aren't we raising the dead to life? Is a lack of fasting one of the primary reasons?

As I've listened to testimonies from Christians who heal the sick and raise the dead, I've found that each of them has one thing in common: they fast on a regular basis. It's part of their lifestyle.

Scripture talks about when we fast, not if we fast. "And when you fast, don't make it obvious, as the hypocrites do, for they try to look miserable and disheveled so people will admire them for their fasting. I tell you the truth, that is the only reward they will ever get" (Matthew 6:16, NLT). Fasting and prayer should be a normal part of our lives according to Matthew 6.

Also, self-control is a fruit of the Holy Spirit (Galatians 5:22-23). Fasting is one important way that we can grow in this fruit. Fasting requires saying no to the flesh and yes to Holy Spirit.

What we feed and yield to in our lives becomes stronger. The more we feed and say yes to the flesh, the stronger it becomes. The more we say no to the flesh, the weaker it gets. The more we feed our spirit with the Word of God, the stronger it gets.

We should rule over our stomachs and our flesh; our stomachs and our flesh should not be ruling over us.

Starving the flesh is a powerful, spiritual tool. Feasting on the Word of God is an amazing way to combat physical desire for food and to fill one's self spiritually.

I heard a testimony from a pastor who received a phone call to cast a demon out of a person. When the pastor arrived and attempted to cast the demon out, he was unable to. The demon manifested, spoke through the individual, and said: "You're too full to cast me out." The pastor said that he wouldn't have any demon shaming him.

The pastor went home and fasted for three days. Then, he returned. After commanding the demon out of the man, it went with no trouble. I wonder what demons are comfortable around us due to our "fullness."

## First Fasting Experiences

I've had different experiences with fasting. I've failed miserably. I've completed a fast. I've also given up things other than food as God led me to. However, true fasting means giving up food, whether all food or only certain foods, for a period of time.

God wants to fill us spiritually, and He wants us to master our flesh. Christians should be good at saying no to their flesh. As we empty ourselves physically, God has more room to fill us with Himself.

One of the first times that I fasted was when I went to Brazil in 2014 on a mission trip. I didn't plan on fasting, but a prophetic man in my church told me that I needed to fast on the first day of the trip. Then, another Christian man said that he was going to fast every other day while we were gone. God called me to fast on the opposite days that this man would be fasting. Then, someone would always be fasting throughout the whole trip.

It took others initiating this and committing to it to help me also choose to fast. Don't you love how God uses the body of Christ to help us? Together, we can accomplish so much more. And, where one is weak, another is strong.

God helped me successfully fast every other day on that trip, and honestly, it didn't even seem hard to do. The trip was awesome! It was as though I got 10 years' worth of spiritual blessings and breakthrough packed into two weeks! I know that I would not have received all of that if I hadn't fasted.

Even if you don't want to be seen fasting, God will often have you around others that will notice that you're not eating. A Brazilian lady who cooked for us was concerned about me not eating one particular day. We were scheduled to climb up some "mountain," which turned out to be a hill. The woman said that the altitude can change drastically and that I needed to have strength for the journey. I replied, "God is stronger." She smiled and said no more. I had no physical problems while fasting on the trip.

I once thought that I would fast for 7 days. I think that I wanted to be able to know and say that I had done it. That is not the right motivation. I failed miserably. I think that I ate after only 1½ days. God didn't call me to that fast; I tried to do it with a wrong motivation. Motivations are important.

Another time, I felt led by God to fast for three days. I was to speak at a tent revival that week. I truly desired to fast for the entire 3 days, but on day 2, when I went to stand up, the room seemed to be spinning. Then, I started wanting food. The more I thought about food, the more I wanted it. I gave in and ate on day 2. Those are some of my "failures."

Every fast is an opportunity for growth. Even through the fasts that I didn't complete, I learned something. Nothing is wasted when it comes to fasting.

God has stirred me to fast for specific reasons. Of course, obedience to God is a good enough reason. Sometimes, we know why God calls us to fast, and sometimes, we don't. It seems easier for me to fast when there's a specific purpose and timeframe in mind.

For instance, I planned to visit a family member who was in great spiritual bondage. God wanted me to do a lot in the natural realm and in the spiritual realm on that trip. God prompted me to do what many call a "Daniel fast." Daniel said that he didn't eat anything pleasant for three weeks (Daniel 10:3, NKJV).

I can't say that I didn't eat anything pleasing, but I did refrain from eating any meat, salt, processed foods, dairy, and sugar outside of what is naturally in food. I mostly ate vegetables, fruit, and nuts. Potatoes were a staple for me.

On day seven of those 21 days, I was really struggling. I craved all sorts of things: my favorite chips, meat, and many other foods. I knew that if I could just make it to the next day, I could persevere. Sometimes, you just need to get through that day. Sure enough, the following day and subsequent days were not so much of a struggle.

I believe that a huge breakthrough happens after completing the 7th day of a fast. On two different occasions, the 7th day seemed to be a turning point during the fast.

With the grace of God, a strong motivation and resolve to complete the fast, and a specific purpose in mind, I was able to complete that 21-day fast. By the way, I had never tried to go without salt, sugar, meat, and dairy for any length of time prior to that. I had wondered if it was possible to go straight into 21 days without first trying it for 3 days, 7 days, or some shorter period of time. But when God calls you to something, you don't need to do a trial run. There is grace for whatever He calls you to do. His grace is key; it is sufficient.

In 2018, God prompted me to do a seven-day fast prior to the day known in the United States as "Halloween." On that night, many adults and children wear a costume and dress as someone or something that they aren't. Many of the costumes are of dark characters or things such as witches, ghosts, etc. There's a tradition where children go to the doors of strangers' houses and say "trick or treat" in hopes of getting candy.

Do you want your children asking for a trick or a treat just to get a few pieces of candy? What does this open up children to spiritually when they put on these costumes? And what kind of tricks does this open them up to? The devil looks for legalities, and this has been a great way for the devil to get legal access to children. Legally, the child did ask for either a trick or a treat over and over. The natural precedes the spiritual.

Interestingly, the devil has many people dressing as people that they aren't all throughout the year.

Many churches have hosted events for the children to dress up and receive candy. I've heard them say that they are providing a safe alternative for children. It's sad when the body of Christ is in deception, but this is changing.

I've heard several testimonies about what goes on behind closed doors on Halloween from people who have come out of Satanic activity. Some were witches, warlocks, etc. Much preparation took place by the Satanists leading up to Halloween. They recounted stories of kidnappings, torture, murder, sacrificing babies, and other kinds of evil taking place behind closed doors on the night of October 31.

Think about the time when Pharaoh, king of Egypt, or Herod, king of Judea, had babies killed (Exodus 1:15-22 and Matthew 2:16). That activity was demonic. The devil is still up to the same sorts of evil. Who do you think is behind abortion? It's not God.

I once heard about a Christian man on a plane. He was sitting next to another man who told the flight attendant that he would not be eating or drinking on the flight. He said that he was fasting against Christian pastors and their marriages. He was a Satanist. Since our enemy Satan understands the power of fasting and is trying to use this against us, why aren't we using fasting against him?

So, God prompted me to go on the offense rather than sit on the defense for the 7 days prior to Halloween. God wanted me to do this through fasting and through my authority and words about what would not happen leading up to or on Halloween. Why wait and act after bad things have happened? When we know that the devil has evil planned, why don't we use our spiritual weapons to stop him?

During day one of those seven days, my monthly cycle came. Honestly, I felt very weak that day, but once I got through that day, the following days weren't as difficult.

Some friends of mine invited me over to celebrate a birthday during that fast. I told my friend that I could come but that I wouldn't be eating. She knows from being around me that fasting is a part of my life. She asked if I could ask the Lord if I could eat this one meal.

She didn't know how long I was fasting or anything like that. I simply told her "no." I knew that I must stand my ground. They had all of my favorite foods at the birthday celebration, but the Lord gave me a determination to not eat, and I didn't.

During those 7 days, I planned to consume only two things: water and communion. By communion, I'm referring to once a day having a sip of pure, unsweetened grape or cranberry juice and a small piece of pure, unsalted cracker or bread in honor of Jesus' blood and body that were sacrificed for our freedom.

There are a couple of fasting principles that I learned from Myles Munroe that really helped me during the 7 days. First, he said to speak to your stomach if it starts talking to you. Our stomachs "growl" and let us know when they want to be fed. Mr. Munroe said that he would speak to his stomach, "Stomach, you aren't going to tell me when I'm going to eat; I'll tell you when you're going to eat."

I did this too. It was very empowering. Take authority over your stomach. Don't let your stomach control you; you control it.

He also talked about how much of our days and our lives have been spent thinking about our next meal. Sometimes, we finish one meal, and we're already trying to figure out the next one. What eternal benefit will there be for all of the time that we've spent on physical food?

Another tool that I learned from him was to use and quote out loud a specific verse anytime that I felt hungry or struggled during a fast. "Man does not live by bread alone but by every word that proceeds out of the mouth of God" (Matthew 4:4). It's not physical bread that will sustain us but rather God's words. Quoting that verse was invaluable to me during the 7-day fast. I used that verse every day – often, multiple times each day.

Fasting is a spiritual battleground. This is why we must use spiritual weapons such as the Word of God and other tools in Ephesians 6 when we're fasting. There's much to be won, so Satan will not want you to complete your mission. As you are winning, guess who is losing?

The other truth that I often quote when fasting is: "Your grace is sufficient for me" (II Corinthians 12:9). There's always a grace for anything that God calls us to.

Since I knew that I had given in to temptation during a previous fast due to feeling dizzy and weak, I spoke against those things before I started this 7-day fast. I declared, "I will not get dizzy, weak, or anything else negative during this fast. This fast will not be hard; it will be easy." It's helpful to take authority over things that you know may try to come against you.

It's also important to declare victory in advance. "I will complete this fast with the help of God. No weapon that forms against this fast will prosper."

With God's grace, God's Word, and other tools and declarations, I completed the 7-day fast! This was a true miracle for me. I actually felt that I could've gone longer. I didn't even feel weak on day 8; I felt very strong.

I noticed that sometimes when the stomach didn't have food in it, I didn't always go to sleep as easily. Yet, no matter how much sleep I did or didn't get, I never felt weak or tired the next day. Again, God's grace is sufficient.

I know that much evil was not able to take place that October 31 as I obeyed God and used my authority and my weapon of fasting. It's time for Christians to go on the offense!

Is God calling you to fast? When will you start?

What breakthroughs await you on the other side of fasting?

Are you walking in your gifts and callings? Do you even know what those are? If not, is a lack of fasting holding you back? Is something else holding you back?

Your destiny awaits you on the other side of fasting. Dead people being raised to life await your fasting. You releasing the gifts inside of you to the world are on the other side of your fasting. Increased freedom and joy are on the other side of your fasting.

What will you commit to right now in this area?

None of these fasts that I've told you about would compare with the next fast that God called me to.

# 14
# 40 Days On Water Only?

I was recently at an event in Orlando, Florida, where thousands of people made various commitments. Some committed to go to the nations; some committed to adopt a child; and even more committed to fast.

I was fasting during the day of the event. The woman next to me kept offering me food. Thinking that she would stop offering me food if she knew I was fasting, I told her that I was fasting. She then told me that it is dangerous to fast.

I get extremely tired of believers acting like it's dangerous to fast. I've about had it with people telling me not to do things that God wants us to do. People listen to the world and the flesh way too much. Not fasting is the easy thing to do. God wants us to know the strength that He gives us when we fast.

Two days after this event, I was watching a video. As I listened to testimonies from a man who has completed two 40-day fasts, I was stirred. I said to the Lord, "If this is something that you want me to do, then let me know."

Be careful what you say. God immediately said, "I'm calling you to fast for 40 days." I told Him that with His help, I would. He said that this was to be a water-only fast.

I read today about Moses' and Elijah's fasts (Exodus 34 and I Kings 19). Moses was on the mountain with the Lord for 40 days with no food or water. Fasting with water should be easier.

I don't pretend to think that I can do a 40-day fast or a 1-hour fast without depending on God.

The following is my journal from that fast. I've left it in its authentic format and have edited very little, as I feel that it's important for you to hear the unadulterated experiences and thinking that I had throughout my journey. Some of the information may seem redundant or even contradictory, but these are the thoughts that I had. It's written as though it is to an audience, as I sensed at the time that God wanted me to document the experience for others.

<u>Fasting Journal</u>

Day 2: Today is day two of 40. It's towards the end of February 2019, and my fast will not be completed until April.

I marked the days on my calendar so that I will know where

## Stolen Identity

I'm at on any given day. Rather than putting "day 1 of fast," I put "40 days remaining," "39 days remaining," etc. I wanted to do a countdown versus a counting up. I want to focus on how much remains, not how much I've already done. It helps to know that there's an end in sight. This is temporary.

I've been watching other videos online and hearing what others have experienced while fasting. I'm hearing that it's a detox for the body. I've also heard about a pastiness on the tongue, sometimes a small rash on the skin that doesn't last long, weight loss, low energy, clearer focus, etc. Mostly, I'm hearing that it is totally possible!

Why do people freak out over fasting for even 1 day? Fasting for 40 days without water is possible if God calls you to it. God hasn't called me to that one this time, but I have heard testimonies of others who have done it when God called them to. God's grace is sufficient.

Why have I heard throughout my life things like, "You'll die after a week or so without water?" Then, many seem to think that you need to consult a doctor, a man on earth, before doing what God in heaven tells you to do. When did people start believing that finite men in the medical profession know more than the Creator of the universe Himself?

I'm stirred in a good way right now. I will write updates as God leads me to.

I'm glad that my monthly cycle started yesterday on day 1. This was the hardest day when I felt weakest on my previous 7-day fast, so I'm glad that day is over. I'll be interested to see what this is like having two cycles during the 40-day fast.

I've already declared victory. I'm not going into this with an "I'll wait and see what happens" mentality. With God's help, there is no reason why I can't complete this. I've taken authority over my body and have told it that we will complete this 40-day fast in Jesus' name.

I'm reminded that the Word of God is our weapon. It was Jesus' weapon during His fast (Matthew 4:1-11). I believe that God's words, along with the fact that Moses was in the presence of God for 40 days, are what strengthened Moses during his fast.

I've been in the Word and plan to continue to each day. I've also saved some videos of fasting testimonies on my phone so that I can watch them at any time.

My plan is to take one day and one moment at a time, always depending on God's help.

Some think that you need to build up to a longer fast. I don't necessarily believe that. I didn't have to build up to the 21 days of eating only natural foods. If God calls you to something, He will help you do it, period. I've seen this for myself. His grace is what I'm counting on the most. His grace is so wonderful. He is so faithful. I trust Him with this.

I have wondered if I have enough weight on me for this length of time, but I know that I will only lose the amount that God wants me to lose and that is available to lose. I don't need to compare my journey with anyone else's. I simply need to trust God, so trust I will.

Day 5: I haven't had any major struggles thus far. I'm very aware though that I have many days remaining on this fast. With that in mind, I seem to be conscious of conserving energy. I think it helps that I had previously done a 3-day and a 7-day water-only fast, not because it built up endurance, but because it enabled me to know what negative symptoms can try to come when fasting.

I knew that declaring things and using my authority ahead of time makes a difference. For example, I declared, "This fast will not be hard; it will be easy. I will not get dizzy, weak, or anything else. God's grace is sufficient for me." I learned through previous fasts that it's better to speak to these things ahead of time, rather than waiting until they try to come.

One man who did a 40-day water-only fast said that he would remind himself that this is temporary and will pass. This was great advice.

The main thing thus far has been taking my thoughts captive. As soon as a thought of food, an image of food, or a smell of food comes, I shut those thoughts down immediately and refocus on "40 days." Satan wants our thoughts.

"If you do more than 7 days, you will have gone further than before" is one thought that has come. Another is, "21 days would be good." No, 8 days or 21 days is not what God has called me to.

Don't accept anything less than full victory in your mind. Take those thoughts captive. "40 days" is something that I keep in my mind continually any time that any thought comes to me about food or doing anything less than 40 days. "I can do this; I will be victorious with the help of God." These are things that I tell myself. Also, I've felt led to thank God each day for the fast and for His grace for the fast. I'm very aware that I can do nothing apart from Him.

I don't want others to be aware of this fast. I dress modestly, so I'm not too concerned about people asking me about weight loss. However, it's still very early.

I don't typically exercise a lot, but I do like to get my heart rate up and do some muscle toning once or twice a week. Could I still exercise during this fast? I think so.

I heard of another woman working out daily during her 40-day water-only fast. I don't know how much extra weight she had on her at the beginning of her fast. At this point, I'm taking it moment by moment, day by day. I don't feel a strong compulsion to exercise or put myself in a situation that might make victory more difficult for me.

God prompted me on day 3 or 4 to get rid of all food temptations that were in my apartment. This included cookies, pizzas, chips, and ice cream – basically anything that would be easy to eat or pop in the oven that might be something I would crave. I sensed that I shouldn't delay, so I took those food temptations straight to the dumpster.

On night 2 or 3, I had a dream. In it, someone convinced me that it wasn't a big deal to eat some cookies, so I ate them. As soon as I did, I was filled with regret. This was definitely a warning from God to not let others influence me. This is one primary reason why I believe that you shouldn't tell others when you are fasting. At least 5 different times, a Christian has tried to get me to eat during a fast.

Please, never encourage someone to eat when they're fasting. Do you think that their flesh wants to fast? If you encourage someone to break a fast that God has prompted them to do, you are basically partnering with the devil. Three different times, people have told me that it is dangerous to fast. They were acting as though I was going to pass out or die from fasting.

In one sense, fasting is dangerous. It's dangerous for the devil. Fasting enables us to conquer him and to take back what is ours. Since some things are only accomplished through prayer and fasting (Matthew 17:21, NKJV), certain victories will not be won unless we go without food.

Although I am drinking water, I don't feel very thirsty, so I'm not drinking as much as I typically would. When my mouth feels dry, I drink. If I feel hungry, I drink more. I don't seem to need as much water. I like keeping my vessel as empty as possible. Knowing that Moses and Jesus fasted without water for 40 days, I'm not trying to overdrink water.

At the same time, God told me that I could have water, which I am thankful for. He knows what each of us is ready for.

I listened to a testimony from a man who fasted from food and drinks, including water, for 40 days. And no, he didn't die. It's a myth that we can only go 7 or so days without water. This man dealt with all kinds of demonic attacks and was bedridden for part of that time. God sustained him though. If God calls you to something, He will sustain you, period.

If others have done it, there's no reason why you or I can't. I've even heard testimonies of nonbelievers who have fasted for 40 days on only water. One man wanted healing in his body, and he got some healing through fasting.

I'm excited. I believe that this fast is connected to my destiny. More doors will open for me, and I will walk in greater power after this. I also believe that my body and my soul need a detox. I will be freed and cleansed of things that I don't even know that I need cleansing and freedom from.

On one woman's 31$^{st}$ day of fasting on water only, some parasites passed through her body during a bowel movement. I believe that these were demons. Imagine if some things only come out after 40 days. It took 31 days for those things to be starved and then expelled from her body. Imagine what we have been holding on to for years without even knowing it. As the Word says, some things only come out by prayer and fasting.

Let's do this! And I believe in you! You can do this! Whatever God calls you to do, do it! No excuses. If He wants you to start with one meal, one day, 3 days, or whatever, start.

In some ways, fasting is like a muscle to exercise. The more you do it, the stronger you get. It can be easy to get a little freaked out the first time or two if you've never said no to your stomach and to any side effects that try to come through fasting. But, once you know that those are momentary discomforts and that you can tell them to leave, it gets much easier.

Again, using the Word of God is a must. "Man does not live by bread alone but by every word that proceeds out of the mouth of God" (Matthew 4:4). I continue to use this verse in any moment of temptation that tries to come.

Fasting should be a normal thing. Christians should be good at saying no to their flesh. I wish that I had heard more Christians sharing testimonies about fasting. I believe that this is changing.

Most things that I've learned have not been through a physical church but rather through my personal relationship with Jesus. He speaks things to me directly and gives me a hunger to learn more. Through that hunger, I search for things. He leads me to conferences or to testimonies online from others who have a revelation in a particular area. If you don't have a personal relationship with Jesus and would like to have one, please refer to the end of this book, "Prayer for Salvation."

I want to see believers operate in true power and authority that Jesus paid a very high price for. We should be making a spectacle of demonic principalities and powers, not the other way around. It's time for the church to arise!

Day 7: Several hours after I said that I hadn't struggled on day 5, the struggle came, and it continued into day 6.

I felt hungry and irritable. I was not feeling strong. For some reason, my teeth felt very sensitive, and my left wrist was hurting. I don't know if those things were connected to the fast or not. I kept reminding myself: "40 days." This is not permanent.

It was a must for me to get in the Word and to read it out loud. God has been leading me to Psalm 3, which says that He is our shield. It also says that He sustains us.

Day 7 has been great compared to the last two days. I haven't felt that I was in a nonstop battle. I've had such peace. When I did struggle, I just tried to focus on getting through that day.

I haven't been focusing too much on how many days remain since more than 30 days could seem like a lot. I realized once I started this week that I have 5 weeks remaining. This sounds doable, so I like the idea of a weekly countdown. I continually remind myself multiple times a day: "40 days." I'm trying to keep my mind on completion.

I have had thoughts of food, but I don't dwell on them. I've already looked online regarding breaking the fast. I have plenty of time to figure that out, but I do want to use wisdom. One man said that he would mix water with yogurt in order to "wake up" his digestive system. I think of it as a baby beginning to eat. Start slowly and introduce gentle things to a new stomach. God will show me the way.

Yay for victory thus far! And yay that God will sustain me for the remaining 5 weeks!

Day 8: It seems that every time I mention that I have a good day or that I'm not struggling, all hell breaks loose. This morning, I woke up feeling nauseous and weak. I decided to drink more water in an effort to feel stronger.

I got in the Word, did some light housework, and took a shower even though my body seemed to be fighting against me.

I began to brush my teeth, and that's when it happened. I hadn't even gone to the back of my mouth. I immediately felt the need to vomit and did. A little bit of greenish stuff came up. Some might say that this is bile; I believe that it is deliverance.

I sat down after that and then vomited a watery, light yellow substance. I felt better afterwards. The nausea was gone. I left for work and prayed that no vomiting would happen at work.

Many years ago, when I was deep in sin, I began to feel sick. I then vomited something green. God later revealed to me that what came up was completely demonic.

As much as I hate vomiting, I'm thankful for whatever breakthrough I'm having today. Never give up, as your breakthrough is just around the corner.

It's midday. I've felt weak, and my mouth has been dry. I drank some water, but I'm trying not to overdo it, as I think that I drank too much water leading up to the vomiting this morning.

I wanted to leave work early today to go home and rest after getting irritated from an issue on the computer, but God said, "I've got you; you can do this." So, I press on and trust Him.

I'm scheduled to go out of town for the next two days for training. I'm trusting God to keep me strong during that time.

I'm learning that each person will have their own unique experience when fasting. One person said that you don't feel hungry after the first 7 days. That has not been true for me. Another said that the first 10 days and the last 10 days were the hardest for him. I don't know about that yet, but I do know that God's got me. He sustains me, and His grace is sufficient for me always.

Day 9: I thank God that I didn't vomit this morning. I'm out of town and feeling great. One day at a time. 5 weeks – I can do this!

Besides the first day or two, tonight was my first bowel movement. Imagine how much waste our bodies are carrying if it took 9 days on water before this came out. How much junk is in us? How badly do we want total freedom?

I'm wondering if everyone should be doing 40-day fasts every so often to clean out their systems physically and spiritually. I believe that this fast is cleaning out organs that have had stuff stored away for years.

My monthly cycle is lasting longer than usual. There isn't much being released, but this is day 9, and it's still not totally done. After about day 4, the coloring got much darker and has remained a very dark color.

In class today, they were passing around a bag of candy. I refrained from eating any. Then, the instructor came in with hot food and a strong smell of French fries. I've had to get used to being around food. I've had a resolve to say no to these things.

Day 11: I thought about food today and was making a list of things that I could make later. Not a good idea. I continue to stay resolved though to "40 days." "Less than a month to go." "Less than 5 weeks." "I can do this." I refuse to settle for less than total victory.

I had another bowel movement this morning. I'm happy when this happens, as I feel it is bacteria, toxins, and demonic stuff that my body is getting rid of. It feels like victory.

I've had an unusual feeling in my lower back that I've never felt before. It's unpleasant. I'm hoping that it's just the toxic stuff working its way out of my system.

In some ways, I'm glad that I'm at work in order to stay busier and keep my mind off the fast. The weekends are a nice break though too.

I get winded easily by simply carrying a few items inside from my car. Maybe all of my organs are in a different mode with this fast. I haven't felt any dizziness. I make a point to stand up slowly and wait a few moments before I begin walking.

Almost 25% done! (Apparently, math skills are affected when fasting, as I was already more than 25% done at this point.)

Day 13: I wish I could say that this fast is easy, but it feels like an eternity. Yesterday, I was so irritable. In the morning, I was glad to go to work to keep myself occupied. Halfway through the day, I felt miserable and wanted to go home.

There's an uneasy feeling in my stomach that is similar to nausea, but it's pervasive. It feels the worst when standing. Sitting is a little better, but lying down seems to be the best position to minimize the discomfort.

I try not to think about food, but the mind wants to think about food. I had read that the hunger completely goes away within a certain number of days: 3, 7, etc. I'm on day 13, and it's hard not to think about food. Maybe it's not a physical hunger. Maybe it's mental, but it's still there, and it's still a battle.

I'm trying to take one day at a time. "Just get through today," is the best thing to do, because frankly, still having 4 weeks left can sound like a long time. I remind myself that I lived in an extremely toxic environment for 18 years; surely, I can manage 40 days of this.

I feel dissatisfied with almost everything at this point. I want to be positive and embrace and enjoy each day fully, but it's a struggle. Typically, certain movies are really enjoyable for me, but I'm almost tired of movies.

It's my Sabbath today, and I'm not sure what I'll do for the rest of the day. I pulled out my adult coloring book and colored pencils. It's been months since I touched either of those.

I just want this fast to be over. One day at a time. I don't want to give up or in. I want to make it to the finish line.

I ordered and received a book on fasting and prayer. This

author has completed multiple 40-day fasts, so I'm hoping that this book will keep me encouraged and motivated.

I don't like feeling miserable. I guess this is part of dying to self. I'm sure that God is doing great things in me, but it's hard to know or see what the fruit is when you're in the middle of it. I'm sure a testimony is being birthed though.

One day at a time: I have to tell myself this over and over. Just get through today. If I look too far ahead, it feels like too long to do this. I am confident though that God's grace is sufficient for me.

I feel that it's important to document in detail my journey, particularly as a woman. The testimonials that I've read from men don't discuss too much of the struggle or "feelings." I suppose that men are not wired the same and don't have as many emotions to deal with. I find it helpful to know the details as a way to not be surprised or fearful if things happen.

12 days down (today isn't over yet); 28 to go. I can do all things through Christ who gives me strength.

Day 14: The last couple of days, I've woken up with extremely dry eyes and a dry nose. Thinking that it would lessen the dry eye feeling, I took my contacts out, but that didn't help.

I haven't been drinking much water for a couple of reasons. When one feels nauseous, putting anything in the body can make it feel worse. Plus, I've been hearing the Lord tell me not to drink too much water. Basically, I'm starving all of the bad stuff in me.

The worst part is the queasy feeling in my stomach. If it weren't for that, everything else would be fine. Thinking that it will alleviate the queasiness, I find myself hoping to have a bowel movement. It's strange because I have that queasy feeling for an hour or two, and then, it seems to magically go away. I don't vomit or have a bowel movement, yet that feeling comes and goes sporadically. Sometimes, it lasts for hours.

I try not to think about food, but memories of every enjoyable meal I've ever had seem to come rushing in at various times. I keep hearing and am trying to practice, "Just get through this day." This makes the whole thing seem less overwhelming. My mind still races ahead at times though.

I've been coloring in my adult coloring book this weekend.

## 40 Days On Water Only?

It's been a good way to clear my mind and distract me from the fast. I seem to alternate between coloring, reading, watching a movie, journaling, and sitting outside for fresh air.

The pasty tongue that comes with fasting and detoxing is awful. The taste is so bad that I brush my tongue multiple times a day. I've read that this is a normal and good thing that your body is getting rid of bacteria and toxins. The bad thing is that one has to be very careful when brushing his or her tongue and roof of the mouth. Because of the gag reflex, I have to be extra cautious not to brush too far back on my tongue. I want to get rid of the taste on my tongue, but I also don't want to make myself vomit. Oh, the joys of fasting!

Tomorrow, I'll go back to work. I hope that I'm less irritable this week. I was in the worst mood on Friday.

I have to stop myself from jumping too far ahead. I've already been looking up how to break the fast and what foods and amounts I should have. God will guide me. His grace is sufficient.

I don't own a scale, but I have looked at myself in the mirror without clothes on. I still see a couple of areas where there is extra that can be lost. Even if I don't see extra, I trust God.

Nonetheless, I have wondered what I will look like by the end of this. Hopefully, people won't notice the weight loss.

I hope to work through this fast until the last couple of days. I took off work the first two days, and I plan to take off the last couple of days also. I'm trusting God for the strength to get me through. I'm sure that He'll also guide me in meal preparation for breaking the fast. He's always been faithful, and I know He will continue to be.

One person said that you should include other believers in your fast; my spirit doesn't resonate with this. Believers, with the exception of a few people thus far, have been the worst when I've fasted in the past. If God leads me to include someone, I will, but if not, I'm not trying to bring any unnecessary spiritual warfare into this. God's got me.

Day 15: Jesus! Fasting is no joke! I've been dry heaving (trying to vomit with nothing coming up) the past couple of days.

I went to work today, but I felt awful. I felt like I was about to vomit at my desk, so I quickly grabbed the garbage can. After dry heaving, I went to the bathroom where a bit of watery, green stuff came up. This happened twice today.

I feel dehydrated, so I want to drink water. But if I drink water, it makes me want to puke.

I had thoroughly brushed my tongue this morning, but within two hours, my tongue felt so pasty that the taste in my mouth made me want to vomit. It seems like everything is a no-win situation.

Today was horrible. I texted 5 or 6 Christian friends and asked them to pray for me. I only told them that I was in a spiritual battle. I'm trying to quote the Word and read it as I know that this is the weapon that Jesus used when fasting.

I went to the restroom today, and when I went to stand up, I was extremely weak and had to sit back down and rest. I'm not trying to draw attention to myself, but I know that I'm walking very slowly the few times that I do get up to go to the restroom. One of my coworkers asked me today if I was feeling ok. I said that I was feeling a bit queasy but that I was fine.

This isn't supposed to be what happens during a fast. I want to keep this quiet. That's difficult when I'm puking at work and moving much more slowly than normal. I can understand why people have said that it's good if you can go away on a retreat or stay home and away from people during a long fast. I've tried to stay home as much as possible. Work has been the only place that I've been going.

I cannot imagine making it 40 days. I completely understand now why people have broken their fast on day 31, 35, etc. I don't know how they even lasted that long. I didn't expect this to be this hard since the Lord called me to this fast.

It's difficult for me to imagine going another day. Today, God told me to aim for 21 days. That's 7 more days!

I've been dry heaving more tonight since I got home. I can't imagine doing this multiple times a day, day after day. God told me that He would release me from the fast after 21 days. It will take a miracle for me to make it another 7 days.

God told me that I should stay home from work the next three days. Today, I just need to get through today. This has, by far, been the toughest day, and I'm not happy about my coworker noticing that something is going on with me.

## 40 Days On Water Only?

I really wanted to go 40 days. I want complete deliverance for me and my family. I don't want to cut it short, but I will need a tremendous miracle from God to even get to day 21 at this point. I didn't expect to be saying this or cutting the fast this short.

I had read that the fast got easier after the first 10 days – wrong! I suppose that each experience is truly individual. It definitely has not gotten easier. It's difficult to explain the intensity of what is going on. Fasting is serious business.

I've had a lot of acne break out on the top of my back. I suppose that it's part of the detox. My face has been extremely clear. I had asked God to keep my face clear, and He has.

I need to mention something that I forgot to add under day 13. Something hard came to the surface of my skin in a private area. I pushed it out of my skin, and it wasn't like anything I have ever seen or felt before. It was narrow and long – about the length of the pink part of my thumbnail. It was so hard that I literally was able to snap it into two pieces. What was it? Who knows? How long had it been in my body? I'm thankful that it was forced to the surface and out.

I slept some during the day yesterday but didn't sleep much last night. When I took my lunch break today, I fell asleep in my car in a deep sleep. When the alarm went off, I didn't want to go back to work. Sleep took the pain and discomfort away.

The last two hours at work felt like 4 days to get through. I thought the day would never end. I got home and immediately got in bed. I didn't put a movie in. I didn't do anything except lay there. I don't even know what to do anymore. I continue to ask God to help me.

I have the book of Psalms playing out loud in the background as I type this. I want water, but it makes me sick. Am I drinking the wrong kind? Should I have only bought one brand of bottled water for this? Can I avoid this in any way?

Some say that they've drunk liters and liters of water a day while on a long fast; I can barely drink a few sips. Some exercise daily; I can barely go to my car and to the bathroom.

One day at a time. Help me, Lord. I pray that tomorrow is a better day.

Day 16: Well, I survived what felt like a dark night of the

soul. I slept little and was tormented much. I kept my closet light on the whole night.

In the middle of the night, I went to the restroom and had a bowel movement that was almost black in color. I hoped that that would stop the tormenting pain in my stomach, but it didn't.

After going back to bed, I began puking up something that burned coming out of the throat. I have a bowl next to my bed for these moments. There was more dry heaving also. It felt like one of the longest nights of my life. When will it let up? Eventually, I went to sleep.

This morning, I asked God for a better day. He heard and answered. Today has been so much better. I dry heaved once, but for the most part, my stomach has been calm.

I've practically avoided water as it seems to have made my stomach worse. I've only had two small sips all day. It's now approximately 5:00 p.m.

I feel extremely weak. It takes a lot for me to simply go to the restroom. Thankfully, it's not a far walk to my bathroom.

I had to psych myself up for the energy to be able to put on some deodorant and brush my tongue. Standing for even one minute gets me extremely winded and wanting to sit down. I'm ready to get my strength back, but six days remain until 21 days will be complete. I should be able to rest a lot over these next few days at home.

In 3 days, I have an appointment to get my oil changed in my car. I also plan to go to the grocery store for items for breaking the fast. Due to my lack of strength, I plan to use a motorized cart and have the bagger help me to my vehicle. The grocery store and the oil change are the two main things that I will need energy for. Hopefully, I can rest after that for the remaining two days of the fast.

The night before I break my fast, I will prepare food. I plan to go to work on my first day of breaking the fast. I'm not sure if I'll stay the whole day, a few hours, or what. I will see how things go.

I've been thinking more about food today. I've already got my grocery list ready for breaking the fast. I've been craving apples today. It's probably best if I don't think too much about food since I've still got several days to go, but this is how things are currently going for me.

I don't know what I was delivered from last night, but it was something really intense. I cannot imagine what Jesus went through for 40 days. Angels came to take care of Him after that fast (Matthew 4:1-11). I can imagine that.

It's bad when you can't stand your own body odor. Due to a lack of strength, I only briefly washed a few body parts with a wet rag and soap at the sink. I don't know when I'll take a full shower or bath – hopefully, the night before I go to get my oil changed. Right now, I'm trying to enjoy being able to rest at home these next few days.

If possible, I highly recommend not working during a long fast. It would be even better to go on a retreat where maybe you can have someone help you with basic necessities.

I'll be glad to get rid of this awful taste in my mouth from the detox.

Today, I read in my book on fasting and prayer. I also watched the movie *Rocky*. A boxer goes through a lot of training in preparation before his fights. I related to it in the sense that I feel that this fast is preparation for what is to come.

In one sense, fasting is training. The training is not enjoyable at all, but victory comes at a cost.

I continue to need the Lord's grace and help every second. I wish that time would fast forward and that next Monday, day 22, would already be here, but God knows what He's doing. I hope that last night was the worst of this. I trust the Lord.

Day 17: It's been burning when I've urinated the past couple of days. I'm assuming that it's toxic stuff being cleared out. Since I hadn't drank too much water, I've been consciously drinking more today. It still burned the last time that I went. I also had another bowel movement this morning.

The weakness persists, but I slept pretty good last night. I've been playing an audio version of the Bible before I go to sleep. I also kept the closet light off since the previous night was horrible when I left it on.

5 more days. God tells me to just get through today.

I brushed my tongue and my teeth; that has been the extent of my hygiene today.

I'm taking things slowly. I started in God's Word and then read in the fasting book. I'm now watching television. It's hard not to get bored.

I'm craving food or at least a drink. I looked at a recipe for garlic mashed potatoes online today. Then, I looked at a restaurant menu. This probably wasn't the smartest thing to do when I still have 5 more days to go, but that's where I am.

I continue to need God's grace for each second. Thankfully, I haven't vomited or dry heaved today. The shortness of breath and weakness from simply standing or going to the next room are the worst physical issues. The body odor continues. I will be glad to have strength again.

Day 18: I thank God for a really good day. I took a bath today! Believe me that this is huge. I needed it in more ways than one.

Tomorrow, I will venture out for the first time in 4 days. I will need God's supernatural strength to get my oil changed and go grocery shopping.

I've been sitting outside on my patio each day. Getting fresh air and not feeling cooped up are important. I'm able to take in God's creation and clear my head a bit. God has blessed me with incredible weather this week. I'm guessing that it's been around 70 degrees – not hot or cold.

I've been thinking a lot about food and especially about my favorite restaurant.

I figured out that I had gotten dehydrated. My urine has been way too yellow, and it looked like something else dark came out too. It burned. I'm trying to make myself drink more water to get out of that state. I'm also hoping that this will give me more strength.

I haven't dry heaved, vomited, or had a bowel movement today.

I feel somewhat clean for the first time in several days. I have sympathy for spouses of people doing long fasts. The body odor is horrible.

It's approximately 8:00 p.m. After tonight, I have 3 more days. I'm hopeful, and I'm believing God for total victory for the now 21 days. I'm hoping that the worst part of this fast is behind me. This has felt like an extremely long week.

I'm getting to practice taking things extra, extra slow.

My day involves the Word, reading in the fasting book, movies, sitting outside, and looking online – often at food.

## 40 Days On Water Only?

I wish that I could fast forward to the finish line. I want all that God wants me to have though through this fast. I'm thankful that He is the author and the finisher of my faith. He will see me through to the end.

Day 20: I haven't felt like journaling the past two days, but I guess I should document this.

God is so faithful. He gave me the strength and grace to get my mail, get my oil changed, and go grocery shopping yesterday.

Sitting at the oil change place was horrible. I was so miserable sitting upright. The minutes seemed to drag by. The first hour felt like an eternity.

Thankfully, when I arrived at the grocery store, there was a motorized cart waiting at the entrance for me. This made things so much easier. A lady in the checkout line helped put some of my groceries on the counter. Then, an older bagger helped me out to my car. He didn't ask if I needed help. He just took it upon himself to help, which was very kind. I cried on the way home for some reason. I don't like being in a semi-helpless state. It's humbling to say the least.

I vomited once yesterday morning on day 19. It was a yellow liquid – gross and strange. The rest of the day was uneventful.

I continue to be obsessed with looking at food menus online and coming up with things that I want to make. One man who has done several long fasts said that he always ends up buying a cookbook during each fast. I can understand why.

This morning, I woke up around 2:00 a.m. As usual, my eyes were extremely dry. I figured that I should drink some water, so I did and then made myself sit up for 30 minutes to try to let the water settle.

When I got up to go to the restroom, I vomited up the water and a little bit of green stuff. I then started dry heaving, and it was hard to breathe. It's in those moments that I don't think that I can continue. Vomiting is one thing, but when it seems to paralyze your insides and makes breathing difficult, it feels unbearable.

Needless to say, I haven't drunk any more water since then. It's approximately 1:00 p.m. Although I feel like I need water, I don't want to make myself sick, so I refrain.

## Stolen Identity

I sat outside for a bit. I've been in my bed and in my room for too long. Going outside is so needed for the mind. With the help of God, I will get through today and tomorrow. I just want it to go by quickly.

I'm tired of my own body odor. I'm tired of not being able to brush my teeth and tongue without it bringing nausea. I'm tired of feeling weak and watching the laundry pile up. I'm ready to shower and wash my hair. I want to do the things around my place that need to be done. I want to have strength again. Fasting is no joke.

Day 21: Last night was awful. I had a constant feeling of unease in my stomach and was dry heaving and vomiting most of the night.

Since water seemed to make me sick yesterday morning, I felt strongly led to not drink any more after that. I didn't drink any more until 7:00 a.m. this morning, which was approximately 29 hours without water.

I was eager to drink water today and drank a good bit. I never felt fully hydrated though.

God told me that I will be able to work this week, which will be a miracle. I've still been getting winded just by standing.

I felt led to bathe today. Although I want to be clean, the strength to stand, wash, dress, etc., is a lot of energy that I don't seem to have. I did bathe and wash my hair, which was long overdue.

When I got out of the tub and stood to dry off, I felt like I needed to vomit. I have a chair in front of the sink in my bathroom in order to conserve energy and stand less. While wet and naked, I sat there and began dry heaving repeatedly. I had trouble breathing, and nothing physical was coming out. It was awful.

I'm tired of vomiting and dry heaving. If it would just come up and out and be done, that would be fine. But often, there is nothing physical to come up, and the heaving seems relentless. Eventually, I was able to dry off, put some clothes on, and get in bed.

Today, I finished reading the book on fasting and prayer. I also finished coloring a huge butterfly picture in my adult coloring book. It feels good to finish things. I suppose that the timing of those two completions are prophetic.

I currently have 2½ hours until the finish line of midnight. I don't know that I even want to sleep before then. I want water, but since I don't plan to sit up much, I don't feel that I should have any.

I don't necessarily want to get up in the middle of the night to break the fast, but I'll wait and see if I'm awake. I feel led to break it with apple juice. I'll wash an apple, cut it up, and put it, along with some bottled water, in the processor. I will then have some fresh, diluted apple juice.

I've asked God to not allow me to get sick at my stomach at work this week. It's also not the shortest walk to the restroom at work, so I'm hoping for a miraculous return of strength.

Three days after my fast is broken, I'm supposed to serve with a ministry at a prison. We're to go in on Thursday and continue going in daily through Sunday. I definitely need God's strength this week for work and ministry.

I'm thankful for God's grace and strength. With His help, I will reach the finish line at midnight. It hasn't been easy, but I believe that God is bringing great fruit out of this and that I will be able to say that it was worth it.

# 15

## Breaking the Fast

I made it through night 21! Although my initial goal was 40 days, on day 15, I didn't think that I could continue. Making it to day 22 on water only was a miracle for me.

Day 1 after the fast: At approximately 2:00 a.m., I got up, made some apple juice, and drank some of it. Although I felt full, I made myself drink one more swallow. That last swallow was the only portion that didn't stay down.

In this case, listen to your body. If you're full, stop there. Also, wait a bit before getting up. Body movement doesn't help with things going down and staying down. I made myself sit up until 4:00 a.m. to allow the apple juice to digest.

I still don't feel hydrated. My mouth continually feels dry. My eyes were also dry this morning, so I didn't put my contacts back in.

I also dry heaved this morning. Movement and lack of water seem to be enemies of anything staying down.

I chose not to use toothpaste today since it seems to give me a bad taste on my tongue and can add to a nauseous feeling.

One might think that I would be eager to eat today, but I'm not at all. I'm at work with a glass of homemade apple juice, and I feel that I have to make myself drink it.

I really don't want to be at work today, but I feel that God wanted me to come in. Sitting up all day is probably best for digestion of what I will eat.

I don't have an exact plan for today, but I brought the remainder of this apple juice, one pear, and one avocado. I'll be doing good to simply finish this juice.

I really don't feel any hunger. I think that the nutrients in an avocado would be good for me, but I will see how things go. I don't want to push too much onto my system.

I hope to stay seated as much as possible with the exception of restroom breaks. I get so easily winded from standing or walking. I'll be glad when that is gone and I can function normally again.

I want to regain my strength quickly. I carefully choose my steps at this point. It takes me some time to recover after any movement. I hope this will go away quickly.

I've been at work for under two hours, and I'm already thinking of being back in my bed. But, how can I get stronger in bed? I must take one day and one moment at a time.

It's strange how a couple of days ago I was looking up all kinds of food to eat. Now, I am barely drinking juice. The mind and reality can be two very different things.

It's difficult to imagine eating the majority of the things that I was eating before all of this. I'm curious to see how long this recovery will take. And how long will it take for my appetite to return?

I began to heave a couple times at my desk. Thankfully, no vomiting has occurred, and I haven't needed any restroom breaks yet. 4 hours down; 5 to go. I want to lay my head down on my desk, but I'm refraining for obvious reasons.

I just ate half of the avocado, and it was amazing. The apple juice didn't taste good to me, but the avocado was awesome. I hope that this is a sign of my appetite coming back. It was the perfect ripeness and doesn't require much chewing, so I believe that it will digest well. I drank a little bit of water before and after eating it to aid in digestion.

One of my coworkers came to my desk and told me to stand up. I said that I've been trying not to stand in order to conserve my strength. She told me again to stand up. After I stood, she gave me a hug and told me, "Be healed in Jesus' name." She said that she had a dream that I was sick in my body and that God told her to come over and do that. I started crying after she left my desk. God is so good. I could feel God all over that and am thankful for the loving body of Christ. I needed that.

I want this other half of the avocado, but I'll probably wait until the other half has had time to digest. I need to go to the restroom but don't want to get up too soon after eating or drinking anything, so I'm waiting.

It's like I'm a newborn baby having to be so cautious with everything. I feel that this avocado is doing much for me. Of course, the words of faith and power have also strengthened me. Thank you, Lord.

I will be glad to get some protein in me, but I will wait for the Lord's prompting on that. Scrambled eggs are what I have in mind once the Lord says that my body is ready. Although it doesn't sound good to me, I bought some plain, organic yogurt in order to help reline my stomach with good bacteria. I will probably have some of that diluted with water this week.

I just got revelation on the sufferings of Christ. Jesus died more than once for us. His 40-day fast was another type of death. When it was done, angels came to take care of Him (Matthew 4:1-11). We really have no idea what He went through for us. God is allowing me to know another level of His love through identifying with another way that Jesus suffered for us.

I went through a type of death in 2011 that enabled me to understand, at least in some measure, what Jesus went through on the Cross. I discuss that in more detail in my first book.

Now, I'm getting to understand a different type of death that Jesus went through. It's very emotional for me. The suffering was by choice and was out of love and obedience. It's almost too much to comprehend.

Now, I begin to understand the blessing of the suffering. I didn't know what would come from this. I'm sure that there will be more, but I've gotten to experience in some measure another type of death that Jesus went through for us.

The day is almost over! I've got less than 30 minutes to go, and there's been no vomiting! Hallelujah!

Day 2: I felt fine when I went home yesterday. It was chilly in my bedroom, so I bent down headfirst to pick up a blanket and robe from the floor. That was a mistake!

Suddenly, I needed to vomit. It was gross. Green liquid exploded out. It had something mixed in it, but I tried not to look too closely. I was hoping and praying that it was bile or bad stuff and not the nutrients from the avocado.

I went to sleep by 9:00 p.m. and was wide awake by 2:00 a.m. I got up and slowly began eating some yogurt diluted with bottled water. The dilution should help digestion and lessen the richness.

I had to make myself eat it, as it didn't taste good. It seemed to be an endless bowl of yogurt. I eventually stopped. I felt full and didn't want to make my stomach process too much.

I felt that I should bathe this morning, but getting up out of the tub tends to make me feel nauseous. I bathed anyhow.

## Stolen Identity

As I got out of the tub, I dry heaved several times. Thankfully, nothing physical came up.

It's now approximately 10:00 a.m., and the yogurt has stayed down. I have a pear and an avocado to eat today. I don't feel hungry at all. Articles that I've read have talked about slowly increasing the number of calories each day and keeping things simple by not adding too much variety for the stomach to process.

Six hours after I finished the yogurt, I ate a portion of the pear. It seems easier to digest and softer than the homemade apple juice. I didn't even feel that I needed it, but I'm trying to regain my strength. It tastes really good. The yogurt has protein, which should refuel my energy and strength.

I'm back at work today and plan to work tomorrow too, Lord willing. This should be good for me to get used to sitting again for long periods of time and functioning again outside of my bed, particularly since I'm supposed to be doing prison ministry two days from now.

I'm eager to get some laundry and housecleaning done. I'm having to take things slowly and not get ahead of myself though. God told me not to overdo it. I will take one day at a time.

I noticed last night that the body odor continues. I'm so ready for that to be over. That and the taste in my mouth have been awful. I'm waiting to see how long it will be before I smell "normal" and also eat normally again. I'm guessing that I will have a new normal.

My leather purse smells horrible. My metal bowl that I've been keeping next to my bed also smells awful. I never noticed these things before. Fasting intensifies one's sense of smell for both positive and negative smells.

I'm getting much stronger. I made it through the grocery store today with no motorized cart and without getting terribly winded or weak. I also put gas in my car. These might sound like small things, but they are huge considering how weak and winded I've been. I'm so thankful.

Avocadoes and yogurt are amazing! They're making a big difference in my strength level. Avocadoes will continue to be a staple for me.

I smelled French fries while I was out today. One day, I will eat fries again but definitely not today or tomorrow.

I ate half of an avocado and want more. I hope that this means that my appetite is coming back. I'm starting to think of chocolate chip cookies. If I have the appetite tonight, I may have some scrambled eggs.

I'm feeling the best that I've felt since all of this started. The body is a miraculous thing in the way that it recovers so quickly. I'm grateful for my coworker who spoke healing over me yesterday and for my dear friend who prayed for me Sunday night over the phone. Neither knew that I had been fasting.

It's going to be a great week. And thankfully, work hasn't been very busy.

Day 3: What an amazing night last night! After only two days of eating again, I did some laundry, emptied the dish washer, gathered the trash, and straightened the apartment. I also hooked up my new router box. I then cooked and ate some scrambled eggs, which were amazing. It was a very productive evening. I didn't get super winded, and this was the first day in a while that I haven't vomited or dry heaved.

Today, I ate a small amount of diluted yogurt and leftover eggs for breakfast. By the time that I got to work, I was hungry. I devoured a large avocado and wanted more. I waited a couple of hours before eating some grapes. It's 11:20 a.m., and I'm ready to eat more. I have a few multigrain tortilla chips, some steamed broccoli and carrots, and a pear to last me until 5:30 p.m. This may not be enough. I'm ready for more protein.

I'm so thankful for the way that the body rejuvenates so quickly with proper nutrients. I'm not having to walk as slowly, and I have much more energy and motivation. It feels so wonderful. I've also started urinating more frequently and seem more hydrated.

The multigrain tortilla chips were wonderful. This was the first salt that I've had in a while. I chewed the chips down to basically nothing before swallowing. I ate steamed broccoli and carrots with a little salt and olive oil at lunch. I chewed for a while to aid in digestion.

I feel ready for chicken, but God led me to wait on that. I'll probably eat 4 or more scrambled eggs tonight. My body seems grateful for the nourishment.

I believe that I'll be able to eat some of the food that we

serve at the prison over the next 4 days, but I will also bring my own fruit, boiled eggs, and other healthy items to offset anything that I should avoid eating at the prison. I'll use discretion regarding what I intake. I don't want to eat much bread yet. I'll also be careful regarding red meat and any fried foods. And, of course, I'll avoid junk food. I may eat some pizza on the last day. I think a bit of mozzarella cheese will be ok for me to have.

Although I don't care for the taste, I'll try to have some plain, organic yogurt each morning for the rest of the week to aid my system in being healthy. Eggs and avocadoes are definitely my two staples at this point. They're delicious, soft, and healthy. They also require very little preparation.

I wore a different head covering to work today. I didn't think anything about it until one person asked me if I was ok. Maybe she could tell that my face is thinner. After I said that I was ok, she said that I looked sad. Another person asked what was wrong with me and told me that I'm looking weak and that my coloring seems different. I told her that I had been weak but am now feeling much better. She told me to eat some mashed potatoes or rice. She seems to want me to put some weight on. I told her that I'm being careful regarding what I put in my body. I noticed one or two others looking at me today also.

In the days and weeks after breaking the fast, the only other effects on my body were major skin breakout on the top portion of my back, which cleared up in time, and swelling of my feet and ankles. I believe that I was retaining some water. I don't recall exactly when this happened, but I think that it was in week two after breaking the fast. I've heard others mention that they also have had swollen legs after breaking long fasts. I intentionally limited my salt intake and elevated my legs in the evenings. The swelling only lasted a few days and was not painful at all. It was just weird seeing my feet that swollen. The body reacts when you start doing a lot of new stuff to it. The great thing is that it recovers quickly and can handle much more than we've known.

After breaking that fast, I found it much harder to fast for any length of time. Even a 24-hour fast seemed so long and hard. My mind and body didn't seem to want me to put them through anything else anytime soon.

God wants me to have a fasted lifestyle, but this wasn't easy for me in the months after the 21-day fast. I sense that I will end up doing another long fast at some point when God leads. For several months after that fast, I barely went 18-24 hours without food, and even that was a real battle.

I recently had the opportunity to speak on fasting at a church. After I finished, several people said that they were stirred to fast. I know that God wants us as Christians to be disciplined and to use the spiritual weapons that are available to us. Fasting is an important one.

There are a few things that I learned from the 21-day fast. First, it's important to use only one kind of water. My body seemed to reject any change. When the body is empty, it's very sensitive to differences in the water that one drinks.

Also, when one is fasting, it can draw the demonic. The demonic is drawn to empty vessels and would like to fill and occupy those vessels.

During fasting, Satan may come at you with sexual temptation. Myles Munroe has stated that the two strongest desires of the flesh are the physical appetite for food and one's sexual desire. When you deny one strong appetite of the flesh, the enemy may come after the other one. Mr. Munroe said that once you have self-control over these two areas, the devil won't have anything on you.

I experienced strong temptation and lots of sexual thoughts coming to me during my long fast. I later talked with a Christian man who had done a Daniel fast for 40 days. He shared that he struggled not to look at pornography during that time.

We must not allow the enemy to take over the ground that we gain. As you get free in certain areas and Satan loses his grip on you, Satan will try to get you bound in another area.

We must not be unaware of the devil's schemes. Be on guard and armor up fully with all spiritual weapons when fasting.

I've had some great results come from that fast. I definitely have more patience. I'm also better at slowing down. To this day, I'm very fond of many of the pure foods that I ate after breaking the fast: avocadoes, scrambled eggs in pure olive oil, fresh mozzarella cheese, and multigrain tortilla chips. Even plain, organic yogurt grew on me. I'm better at putting healthy items in this temple of the Lord. I'm also so much stronger. The strength came through weakness and dependence on God at a much higher level than before. Most importantly, I'm closer to Jesus after that fast. I'm sure there is more, but those are the things that I'm most aware of. The blessings of the fast have far outweighed the cost.

Seven months later, God has been prompting me to fast more often as I press in to finish this book. I fasted for more than 30 consecutive hours in the last two days, and already, I've seen a huge, positive difference in my motivation level.

While I was fasting yesterday, things started coming to my mind that I could get rid of, so, I put them with the trash. I'm sure that this is further deliverance.

This morning, I took several bags and boxes to the dumpster. Next, I cleaned out my refrigerator and freezer. I then did a return at a store and still got to work early! I can't remember the last time that I was early for work, much less had time and energy to do housework and errands before work. Fasting gives energy and clarity in amazing ways.

Writing and editing this book has been easier while fasting. In fact, you wouldn't be reading this if fasting weren't part of my life. Fasting affects our identity, and it also affects whether or not others come into their identity and destiny through us.

Fasting! Have you fasted? When was the last time? What is God calling you to do now?

Do you need more clarity or more energy in your life? Fasting may be your answer.

Fasting will enable you to walk in your God-given destiny.

Next, God showed me that there were several systems that I was in that were negatively affecting my identity and destiny.

# 16

# Insurance

What systems are in this world? What are the originations of these systems? Why were they set up? What are they meant to accomplish? Are these systems helping or hurting us?

In 2018, God had me thinking about the word "insurance." Insurance is often thought of as a safety net. People get insurance to protect themselves, their loved ones, and their property in case something bad happens. Common categories of insurance include health, automobile, home, life, etc.

God had me specifically thinking about health insurance. Health insurance is a system. Think about the terms "in network" and "out of network" that are often used in health insurance. One is either in the network or out of the network.

So, what all is involved "in the network" or in the system that one joins? Is that system, company, or plan part of anything that is contrary to God's ways? What is a person knowingly or unknowingly uniting with? What does a person come under in the spiritual realm when they sign up for a "plan?"

There are roots to every system. These roots and origins are spiritually important. There is often much in the unseen realm behind everything that we see.

How can Satan get us to depend on someone or something other than God? How can he get us to think that we don't have authority and that we need something or someone else to help us with our health?

Does a person need health insurance? As Christians, we've been given authority over sickness and disease. Of course, the devil doesn't want us to know that we have this authority, much less to use it.

Why would anyone vote for or enact laws that would require its citizens to be part of a health care system and even institute monetary penalties for not being part of that system? This happened in the U.S. There are deep roots to all of these things.

By the way, I had health insurance at the time that God began speaking this to me. I had been in the health care system for many years through my job.

God started reminding me how He has had me use my authority over anything that has tried to come against my health. If you read my booklet *Pain-Free Periods: Yes, It Is Possible!*, you will learn how God has shown me to take authority over anything that is contrary to complete health and living pain-free. After suffering from horrible period pain for over twenty years, God showed me that I didn't have to anymore. In that booklet, I share the details. I've been having pain-free periods for over three years now.

So, since we have authority over all sickness and pain, why would we need to sign up for "insurance" to help with something that we already have authority over?

2 Chronicles 16:12-13, NLT, says, "In the thirty-ninth year of his reign, Asa developed a serious foot disease. Yet even with the severity of his disease, he did not seek the Lord's help but turned only to his physicians. So he died in the forty-first year of his reign."

Hmm, this king died within two years of developing a foot disease even though he consulted the physicians. He went to his physicians but did not seek God. He placed the physicians over God in this area of his life. The disease then took his life within two years.

How many people are not seeking God if an affliction hits their body, their mind, or their emotions? Have we lifted up the medical community and their advice over God Himself and the authority that He has given us?

I'm not saying that one should never see a doctor. This is particularly true for those who don't know or use their authority in this area. I do believe though that the first person that we should talk to regarding our health is God. Ask Him what to do.

There's a problem with having a mindset of first running to man instead of God. God has the solution and will show each person what to do if he or she will ask Him.

God told me that He is my insurance. He also told me that there are things connected to the health care system that are not of Him. He told me to come out of the health care system. This would require faith.

For many years, I had been in a mindset that one should get insurance and that insurance was a good thing. This probably started when I was required by law to get automobile insurance when I got my first car. That may be where the first open door to insurance took place in my life.

There also seemed to be roots of fear that something bad could or would happen if I didn't have insurance. The devil is such a liar. So many decisions are made out of a root of fear. God does not give us a spirit of fear, but rather of power, love, and a sound mind (II Timothy 1:7).

The thinking seems to be that insurance is our security. What sounds wrong about this? Insurance is not our protector or our provider. The Lord Himself is the One who watches over us and provides for our needs. When has God not taken care of us?

I wonder how many times people have died within two years of getting an affliction because they turned only to physicians and not to God. I wonder how many systems in this world have been set up to go against God, His ways, our faith, our authority, and our identity. How many things have we blindly accepted and entered into without any questions?

So, God told me to come out of the health insurance plan that I was in through my job. Even the word "plan" is something to think about; it's like we're planning on something going wrong. We're planning to need the insurance. I wonder what spiritual doors get opened through these systems and plans that we sign up for. We literally sign legal contracts when we come into and under these systems.

Think about anything that has required your signature. What did that signature have you come under and into agreement with legally in the spiritual realm?

God wants me to share with you about prenuptial agreements. Please don't ever have them. Why are you planning for the marriage to end before it has ever begun? If you feel that you cannot trust your potential spouse in the area of money, then do not marry him or her until this is resolved.

God intends for husband and wife to become one in every area – including finances. Prenuptial agreements often specify how to keep property and money separate and in separate names. Prenuptial agreements are not safety nets; they are demonic traps. They legally open spiritual doors for the enemy to come into that relationship and wreak havoc as people sign and put in writing that they will keep things separate. If you don't really want to become one with someone, especially in the area of finances, then don't get married until you get free in this area. Please don't go into marriage afraid or thinking that a piece of paper will protect you. That piece of paper can invite and welcome demonic activity into that relationship. Say no to fear, and say no to systems that are rooted in a spirit of fear.

If you want greater unity in your marriage, make sure that you have both spouses' names on everything. The devil looks for legalities. If you have separate bank accounts, don't think that the devil isn't using that against your relationship and against the oneness that God intends for you to have. It's time to say no to fear and yes to God and His ways. God makes no mistakes, and He loves you more than you can fathom. His ways are always best.

In July 2018, I checked into removing myself from the health "care" system and "plan" that I was in. It was an act of faith. I learned that my job wouldn't let me remove myself in the middle of the year unless there was a "qualifying event," such as getting married, an adoption, etc. I would have to wait until the end of the year to cancel my health "plan." I wasn't happy about this, but this was the legal agreement that I had previously agreed to. It's often more difficult to get out of these systems than it is to get in them, which says something.

At the end of 2018, I cancelled all of my health insurance and life insurance plans through my job. I could feel the opposition in the unseen realm. Choosing faith over fear is not always easy, but the truth is that God has always taken care of me, and He will continue to. My security is not found in a system; it's found in God alone.

Why was I planning on my death through "life" insurance? Maybe life insurance should be called "Payment for Dying." I wonder what we give legal access to in the spiritual realm when we come into these plans and systems.

I knew that there was a law in the U.S. that required taxpaying citizens to show the federal government that they were part of a health care system for the entire year, or else they would have to pay the federal government a penalty. There were few exceptions or exemptions to this law. I had been asked this very question on my tax return in recent years regarding whether or not I had health insurance for the entire year. This began to anger me. I was ready to fight this all the way to the highest court if necessary. Why would a government require its people to be part of a system? And, if you don't comply, you are supposed to pay them money for not being part of it. Basically, you will pay one way or the other.

So, I found a Christian-based minimal health plan at the beginning of 2019 that supported many Godly values and did not support abortion. It was separate from major health care plans. I didn't even want to get it, but I chose that over paying the government anything.

A couple months later, I learned that Congress members under President Donald John Trump had voted on a Tax Cuts and Jobs Act at the end of 2017 that repealed the penalty for not having health insurance. This went into effect for the 2019 tax year. Hallelujah! This just made my life easier. So, I cancelled the Christian-based health "plan."

As my first year without the world's health "insurance" began, I had an issue with one of my ears. It felt like something was keeping it partially closed. I took authority over it, but it didn't seem to open up right away. This was a definite test.

Is it a coincidence that something tries to come against my health as soon as I cancel my health "plan?" God told me that He had me and that I didn't need to go to a doctor.

When the ear issue didn't go away right away, I started wondering if I needed to go to a specialist. These are the natural thoughts that came. Yet, God told me that He had me. So, I continued to stand in faith and not fear.

Fear would have led me to go to a doctor and spend unnecessary time and money. Also, what if they had given me a bad report or a bad diagnosis? And what if I had come into agreement with a bad report?

In time, the ear issue completely went away. I never once went to the world's physicians. Faith works.

I've been without the world's health insurance for over two years, and it's been priceless. I haven't needed to go to a doctor one single time. Living in faith, in my true identity, and in authority, has been awesome. Faith works. Obedience works.

During this time, I once had a slight fever and some congestion. I first took authority over those things by telling them to leave in Jesus' name, and I spoke wellness over myself. I also spoke to God and examined myself before Him.

God directed me to take a couple of over-the-counter medications, so I did. The congestion didn't clear up completely for almost two weeks. I was tempted to go to the doctor, but when I spoke to the Lord about it, He told me that it was not necessary. So, I listened to God.

In time, there were no more symptoms. I am completely healed.

In September 2019, I went to Uganda. This was my first trip to the continent of Africa. In order to go into this area, the country requires you to get a yellow fever immunization. I wasn't happy about getting it because I know that I have authority over things like that.

When I went to the local health department for the yellow fever immunization, they wanted all of my immunization history. The nurse also recommended several other immunizations, which I declined. She then asked me why I didn't want other immunizations besides the yellow fever one.

I made the appointment for a yellow fever immunization, not for anything else. I don't owe any explanation to medical staff regarding what I choose to do or not do with my body. It amazes me when medical staff, who may have a financial motive to want you to get more treatment, try to scare or pressure a person into getting additional, unnecessary treatments, procedures, immunizations, etc.

I believe that it's best to not offer any information or explanation as some will try to change your position or will want to argue. I don't expect someone who doesn't have the same revelation that I have to understand or agree with my decision. I stood my ground and did not get any other immunizations. I also did not offer any explanation of why I wasn't getting them.

This has also happened to me at the dentist office when I refused to allow x-rays to be taken. They asked why. I don't owe any explanation, and I'm not here to argue. I want my teeth cleaned – nothing else. It's interesting that the employees don't even stay in the room during the x-rays, yet they are quick to say that you need to have them done twice a year.

Recently, I visited a new dental office closer to my home. I like to get my teeth cleaned. After advising the office that I did not want any x-rays taken, they refused to serve me. They literally would not provide any type of service without me agreeing to unnecessary x-rays. Since when do patients not have a say-so? I left the office rather than giving up my authority and giving in to unnecessary x-rays. I then left critical reviews of the business on multiple websites. It's time that we speak up about things that aren't right. If no one says anything, these things will continue. The negative reviews got their attention. They called me to ask if there was anything that they could do. I don't care to do business with offices like that, so I never called them back.

Before I got the required yellow fever immunization, I took authority over it and declared that I would have no negative side effects. I also released the blood of Jesus over the shot and declared that I would receive nothing negative through it. After getting the shot, I had no soreness and no negative side effects.

The next opportunity to use my authority and my faith regarding my health came around the same time. Before the trip to Uganda, the group was told by one of the leaders that we were to get a prescription for anti-malaria pills. These were to be taken daily during the trip and for some days afterwards.

I want to use wisdom, and I also want to be respectful of people in positions of authority. However, my body is the Lord's domain, not someone else's. God's thoughts were what I needed to know, and I had no peace about the malaria pills.

I looked up information on the anti-malaria pills. There are different kinds, but all of them are known to have some side effects. Why would I want to have negative side effects when I don't have to?

Also, why would I need to pay money for pills to try to avoid getting something that I already have authority over? And the "medication" that the people from my area would be taking required one to take the pill with a full meal each day.

God told me to fast on certain days of the trip. Taking this pill with a full meal each day would directly go against the fasting that God had told me to do.

As we prepared for the trip, "malaria" kept getting brought up. The pills were talked about as though they were mandatory, rather than optional. There seemed to be a lot of fear surrounding "malaria." This was frustrating to me. Where is the faith?

I didn't feel led to share my thoughts with others at that time, so I didn't. As I talked to the Lord about it, I knew that I wasn't to get the malaria pills, so I didn't.

We hadn't even left our city before the leader asked if I had taken the malaria pill for that day. It was asked as though there was no choice in the matter. I wanted to be respectful. I also didn't want to get into an argument. I sensed that God wanted me to say very little. I simply said, "I won't be taking the malaria pills, but I'm good." There was no response, which was fine with me. I do believe that this leader meant well in wanting to look out for our health.

Before leaving for Uganda, I used my authority and declared out loud that I would not get malaria, yellow fever, or anything else. I also commanded the mosquitoes to stay away from me, and I declared that anything that tries to come near me will get infected with what I carry: the blood of Jesus.

The greater One lives inside of me. I don't go into an area fearing what is in that area. I have no doubt that things such as malaria or anything else negative known to be in an area are from the devil.

There are principalities in the unseen realm that are influencing these things. We as believers have authority over those principalities. God wants us to stop being so naturally minded. We need to discern what is going on spiritually. Malaria or any other name that seeks to steal, kill, or destroy is beneath my feet. I sit with Christ in heavenly places, far above principalities and powers of the devil (Ephesians 1 and 2).

And the Word says that we can move mountains by speaking to them. They will move if we believe (Mark 11:23-25). God gave us dominion over the animals in the beginning; they don't have dominion over us (Genesis 1:28). And anything that was lost in the garden was regained by Jesus after He died and rose again.

It took three days to get to Uganda. Each of those three days, I heard fear-based talk about malaria and about taking the pills to try to avoid getting malaria.

The first night in Uganda, I had my own hotel room. It was awful in more ways than one. The bedsheet was disgusting. And

## Insurance

as I unraveled the mosquito net that is meant to go around the bed to keep the bugs out, there were two live mosquitoes inside the net.

The window to the room had a gap between it and the wall, so, there was seemingly wide-open access for bugs to come in through that gap at any time. Of course, I commanded them to stay out. Nonetheless, it was unnerving to say the least.

So, the window doesn't close fully, and I have live mosquitoes in here with me. The bed is gross. I was separated from my checked bag and am attempting to sleep in my dress that I will be wearing tomorrow. Welcome to Uganda! Talk about being tested. I commanded the mosquitoes to stay away from me. We can speak to the mountain, in this case the mosquito, and it will move, if we believe.

It was a long, awful night. It was hard not to think about the disgusting sheet that was on the bed. It was also hard not to think about the mosquitoes that were already in the room with me, particularly after hearing so much talk about malaria.

God wants us to face these things. It felt like I had demons in the room with me, more so than mosquitoes. I had come into a territory in which the principality in that area uses fear and things in the natural such as malaria in order to get others to bow down to him. I refuse to bow to "malaria" or any other name except Jesus. Malaria, cancer, etc. must bow to the name of Jesus. I don't bow to malaria.

Know that when you take a stand against principalities and powers in the unseen realm, they are aware of it. When you know your authority in Christ and use it, the devil will not be happy. But, we should be telling the devil who the boss is, and it's not him. We've let him get away with too much for too long.

My refusal to yield to fear and "malaria" made that demonic principality very angry. I could sense it. Demons tried to torment me with fearful and intimidating thoughts all through that first night. I could also hear a mosquito buzzing near me.

The choice was mine: bow to fear, malaria, and this principality in this area or stand my ground in faith. I continued to use my authority and commanded the devil and the mosquitoes to go.

I didn't sleep much, if any, that night. Eventually, I was able to kill the mosquitoes that were in the room with me.

## Stolen Identity

Night one in Uganda was truly a test. God helped me to persevere, and no mosquito ever landed on me or bit me.

The next day, I saw that I had anti-bug wipes in my bag. Coming out of mindsets is often a process. I still had brought other things such as bug spray and bug wipes, even though I had chosen not to take anti-malaria pills.

The second morning in Uganda, God asked me, "If you have authority over malaria, why do you need bug spray or bug wipes?" He's right. So, I chose not to use any form of anti-bug products. I used my words, faith, and authority instead.

There was a lot of fear in the atmosphere. People were regularly offering me bug spray, bug wipes, and even bracelets that are supposed to help keep the mosquitoes away. God helped me to stand my ground and simply reply, "I'm good." Malaria talk seemed to be endless.

The Lord helped me to stand my ground and trust the authority that He has given me. After 10 days in Uganda, a few days in South Africa, and me using absolutely no anti-bug anything, guess how many mosquito bites I received on that trip? Zero! Zero! Zero! We have authority! We need to know it and actually use it. The Lord is our insurance.

We can be connected with things in insurance systems and plans that are negatively affecting us without us even knowing it. The devil counts on people not being aware of his schemes. One must know the voice of the Lord and follow it in all things. We are to come out from the world in more ways than one.

A lot of believers have been in deception regarding many systems in the world. I was one of them. God wants the church to arise and take its rightful place. We are to be separate from the world. We don't need the world's systems to provide for us what God has already provided.

Will you ask the Lord now if there is any change that He wants you to make regarding your health, medical decisions, or any insurance plans that you are part of?

Do you believe that God knows better than the world? Do you trust God over the medical community?

Do you know the authority that you have in this area of your health? Will you use it? Are you choosing faith over fear?

Insurance wouldn't be the only system that God would tell me to come out of.

# 17
## 401(k)

The second system that God spoke to me about was also through my job: the 401(k). The 401(k) is a retirement plan in the U.S. Employees put funds into this account to save for retirement, for when they are older. The employer will often match a percentage of what their employees put into the 401(k) account.

The funds come directly out of the person's paycheck and go straight into the retirement account, the 401(k). Rather than having to pay taxes now on those earnings, the taxes are deferred. The person doesn't have to pay taxes on those funds until they are withdrawn, which is often at retirement. Once the funds go into this account, there are very few legal reasons that allow a person to withdraw from this 401(k) account prior to retiring or leaving their job. For some, retirement or leaving their job may not happen for 20, 30, or 40 more years.

I was contributing into a 401(k) the amount that my employer would match. For example, let's say that I was putting $1,000 per year into this account. My employer would match that $1,000, whereby I would then have $2,000 put into the retirement account at year's end, plus any interest that I may have earned on those funds. This sounds wise.

Having a "safety net," an "insurance" for when people retire or get older, appeals to many people. On the surface, it seems good and logical to save for later.

But, things are not always as they seem. What are God's thoughts? God started changing my thinking. He told me that His returns are thirtyfold, sixtyfold, and a hundredfold (Matthew 13:8-9). So, if I choose to trust God with that $1,000, I will get $30,000, $60,000, or $100,000. Hmm. It sounds like God's returns are far better than man's or the government's.

Also, God was working in my heart about the concept of saving. What am I saving for? Isn't life meant to be lived now? And, is fear connected to my mindset of saving for the future? When has God not taken care of me? Why am I not using what He's already given me? Do I think that He will entrust more to me if I'm not even using what He's already given me?

How stale do those funds get when they sit for 20, 30, or

40 years? What really old seasons in my life am I staying connected to through those stale funds?

Would we choose to hold on to and not use our spiritual gifts for 20, 30, or 40 years? Would it make sense to not teach, prophesy, evangelize, etc. for 30 years? Would it make sense to hold on to those gifts that God has entrusted to you and not use them for long periods of time, even decades?

There are many mindsets and systems connected to money that are not of God.

What are the organizations that hold those funds doing with that money? What are they investing in and connected to? Are they connected to and investing in unholy things? What am I now connected to by allowing them to hold those funds?

Do you remember the parable that I mentioned in the prosperity chapter? God used the same one to tell me that He wanted me to get rid of my 401(k) and use those funds.

There was a man who entrusted his money to three of his servants before he went on a long trip. He gave one bag of silver to one person, two bags of silver to another, and five bags of silver to the third. The one with five bags of silver invested his money and earned five more; the one with two bags of silver did the same and earned two additional bags of silver. The one with one bag of silver hid his money in the ground. When the man returned from his trip, he called the servants to give an account for the silver. He praised the two who had used what he gave them, but listen to what he says to the one who buried the silver in the ground (Matthew 25). "Then he ordered, 'Take the money from this servant, and give it to the one with the ten bags of silver. To those who use well what they are given, even more will be given, and they will have an abundance. But from those who do nothing, even what little they have will be taken away' " (Matthew 25:28-29, NLT).

Although investing in the world's system of the 401(k) had sounded wise, God told me that I had been aligned with things that weren't good. What had I been connected to in these accounts where the money was stored? And what other people, who also put money into these accounts, was I connected to?

God also told me that His rate of return is far better and that it was time to come out from the 401(k). He isn't entrusting me with things to hold on to for thirty or forty years. He wants me to use now what He's given me. Yet again, He told me that He's got my future.

I immediately stopped putting funds into the 401(k) plan. I checked into removing the funds that I had already put in, but legally, I couldn't even withdraw those funds until I either retired or quit my job.

So, I literally have funds that I already earned that I now want access to, but legally, they're bound up. This is frustrating to say the least. Do we understand the bondage that we get into when we enroll in these systems? I sure didn't. And these systems hold people captive for years, even decades, until they retire or leave their job.

One level of freedom came when I stopped my contributions. Total freedom from that system came once God called me out of that job.

That job didn't make it easily known that you could withdraw or cash out your 401(k) when you left. They instead promoted leaving the money bound up until retirement. I chose to listen to the Lord and withdrew all of my funds. He showed me that it was an option, and He showed me how to do it.

I'm currently enjoying using those funds. It's great to live life now. There's no need to worry about the funds running out. God's supply line is not limited. His funds never run dry. I will never not be well taken care of when God Himself is my provider and my leader.

It's also great to have total freedom from another system. I am free from mindsets that are contrary to God's ways, and I'm also now free from unholy alliances that I hadn't even known that I was connected to. Freedom! Don't you want to experience more freedom? Words can't describe how free I am and how wonderful it feels.

Why are people planning so much for sickness, death, and retirement instead of fully enjoying their lives now? Why do people let fear of the future cause them to forgo the good things that God wants them to enjoy now? I know Who holds my future, and it's a great future. What about you?

These systems are demonically inspired and are stealing from people. There's much deception involved. It's time to say "no more" to Satan. It's time to come out of these systems and to be smarter than the devil. It's time to come out of unholy alliances and unholy mindsets. It's time for you to enjoy living your life now.

Do you think that any system can help you better than our heavenly Father can? What is God speaking to you regarding 401(k), saving, and retirement? What change is God calling you to make today? Greater levels of freedom and joy await you on the other side of your trust and obedience.

The next system that God spoke to me about has been more difficult to remove myself from than any of the others.

# 18
# 501(c)(3)

In the United States, many churches and nonprofit organizations file paperwork with the federal government and ask permission to form their organization under a 501(c)(3) agreement. This status of being a 501(c)(3) organization enables them to be tax-exempt, which means that they don't have to pay federal income taxes. Also, donors can list their contributions to these organizations on their taxes and potentially owe less taxes for that year.

On the surface, it seems like a good thing. People don't like paying taxes, so leaders of organizations often feel that they've gained something when they get approved for the 501(c)(3) status. Many organizations promote this, are proud of it, and believe that this status helps people want to give more since they will potentially "get a benefit" on their taxes.

I have claimed and listed charitable contributions to 501(c)(3) organizations on my taxes for many years. I gave an accounting to the government of each and every church or nonprofit organization that I had given to and the amount that I had given in order to possibly owe less taxes.

Recently, God allowed me to hear that there are problems with the 501(c)(3) status. At first, I dismissed it. Often, a seed has to be watered before it grows and produces fruit.

Eventually, I looked online and learned that under this designation, one cannot be an "action" organization. Hmm, how is it good to be set up under something that immediately talks about "no action?" Although this may be referring to political action, why would anyone want to align themselves with limitations in their organization or their church? Didn't Jesus pay a high price for our total freedom? Doesn't He want our businesses, our churches, and everything else totally free too?

There's another principle here. What is an organization aligning themselves with when they set up this 501(c)(3)? Did you know that Planned Parenthood, which currently facilitates the killing of unborn babies in the United States, is also a 501(c)(3)? Do you want to be in the same category as Planned Parenthood in the natural or the spiritual realm?

By the way, the name "Planned Parenthood" is so ridiculous

and deceptive. It should be called, "Plans to Kill Your Children and then Let You Live with the Guilt."

God is also dealing with me about my giving being private. Why do I need to tell the government or anyone else who I am giving to? "But when you do a charitable deed, do not let your left hand know what your right hand is doing, that your charitable deed may be in secret; and your Father who sees in secret will Himself reward you openly" (Matthew 6:3-4, NKJV).

I can't help but wonder if we have been unknowingly missing our Heavenly Father's rewards for giving because we haven't been giving privately and instead have been giving an account to the government, expecting the government to reward us by decreasing the amount of taxes that we owe.

Again, do we think that the government's or the world's systems and ways are better than God's? Do we think that the government's "rewards" are better than God's? It's time to put God and His ways back on the throne over all that pertains to us.

God's ways are not man's ways. And God's ways are not necessarily the government's ways either.

Interestingly, churches in the United States are already tax-exempt based upon the way that the tax codes were originally written. Many churches haven't known or understood this, so they've applied for the 501(c)(3) status, thinking that they're getting something.

Actually, they become a "no action" organization and are partnered in the spiritual realm with organizations that murder unborn children. Again, legal documents and legal agreements are signed when these organizations are set up. Sound familiar? What are these organizations giving up when they sign these documents?

Do we need the government's permission to do what God has already commissioned us to do? Do we even need a separate building to have church? We are the church.

Not only is the love of money the root of all kinds of evil, but fear regarding money and taxes is also the root of all kinds of evil.

Maybe you have an organization that is not a church. Maybe you are thinking that you don't want to pay taxes to the government. In Mark 12, Jesus was asked by some Pharisees whether or not they should pay taxes to Caesar. Jesus replied, "Give to Caesar what belongs to Caesar, and give to God what belongs to God" (Mark 12:17, NLT). Is trying to get out of paying taxes a Godly mindset?

How do you know that you are actually benefitting financially as a 501(c)(3)? Do you think that being in an unholy alignment under the 501(c)(3) brings greater blessings than doing things God's way? Are you actually under a limitation that has prevented the full blessings of God from coming into what He has called you to do? Do you want people giving to your work only if they can get something in return from the government? What type of setup is that? Is the government the rewarder, or is God our rewarder?

When God revealed this to me, He told me to come out from all financial transactions with 501(c)(3) organizations. I started researching the organizations that I was giving to on a monthly basis, and every single one of them was a 501(c)(3)! Wow! This was not an easy decision or an easy action to take.

Yet, I trust the Lord. He is telling me to come out of an unholy alliance in the unseen realm. He knows the full ramifications of these things that we are partnered with, and He wants the very best for us. So, one by one, with God's help, I began to cancel my monthly contributions to all 501(c)(3)'s.

God also prompted me to write to some of those organizations and let them know why I was withdrawing my financial support, so I did. Taking a stand is not always easy.

Please seek God about this. I know that there are things in the unseen realm that prevent God's people from walking in their full identity and authority. Are 501(c)(3)'s part of the problem?

God doesn't make us do anything, but He does desire that we trust Him and follow Him in all things. Not conforming is often what we are called to do.

My 2019 tax return was the first year that I intentionally didn't list my charitable contributions to the federal government. Think about those words "tax return." Why have we expected the government to give us a return on what God Himself gives us a return on? And again, why are we telling the government what we should not even be telling our own left hand about? It's time to put God back on the throne in this area. I literally threw away the statements from the organizations that showed how much I had given for that year. That is no one's business but God's. My rewards come from Him, not from the government.

I now try to give in cash when possible so that there's no record of my giving. This is one way that I try to keep my giving private.

I wonder what I've been freed from now that I no longer am partnered with 501(c)(3) organizations and am no longer telling the government how much I have given and where I have given.

What is God speaking to you? What action will you take today?

I find it interesting that each of the three systems that God called me out of involved money and trust. Hmm, are these systems why God's people have not been prospering the way that the Bible talks about us prospering?

# 19

# Wrap-Up

I continue to come out of alignment with things set up to go against my identity and the blessings and the freedom that God has for me. My hope is that through this writing and others, you will do the same and will find the joy and freedom that I have found.

Everything is not always as it appears. Just because something has been widely accepted, that doesn't mean that it's good for us. Many things in this world are actually set up to steal from us and to keep us from learning and being who God made us to be. Many things are set up to prevent us from fully loving ourselves and living the lives that God created us to live.

Are you walking fully in your destiny? Do you know who you are? Are you living completely in your true identity? Do you know why you're here?

Be courageous. Act on what God has spoken to you through this book. As you do, your life will make more sense and will be richer and fuller. Your joy will increase, and others will be blessed through you living out your life's callings.

Today is the day to take back every part of your identity that's been stolen. Today is your day.

## Prayer for Salvation

Do you have a personal relationship with Jesus? If not, do you desire one? Have you felt a tugging on your heart as you've read this book? Do you have a profound sense that something is missing in your life? Do you have conviction over your sins?

"Jesus said to him, 'I am the way, the truth, and the life. No one comes to the Father except through Me' " (John 14:6, NKJV). Jesus is the Son of God. He left heaven, came to earth as a man, and died a cruel death on a cross to pay the price for my sins and your sins. By faith, we can call upon His name. "For 'whoever calls on the name of the Lord shall be saved' "(Romans 10:13, NKJV). I John 1:9, NKJV, states that, "If we confess our sins, He is faithful and just to forgive us our sins and to cleanse us from all unrighteousness."

Salvation, being saved from the penalty of your sins, is a gift from God. It cannot be earned by doing good things. And it will not be withheld from you because you have done bad things. Ephesians 2:8-9, NLT, states, "God saved you by his grace when you believed. And you can't take credit for this; it is a gift from God. Salvation is not a reward for the good things we have done, so none of us can boast about it."

God loves you! "But God showed his great love for us by sending Christ to die for us while we were still sinners" (Romans 5:8, NLT). Jesus and Christ are the same person; sometimes, people refer to Him as "Jesus Christ."

If you'd like to invite Jesus into your heart and have a relationship with Him, talk to Him and let Him know exactly what you're thinking and feeling. There aren't any right or wrong words to use. It is good to confess to Him anything wrong (any sins) in your life currently and any that you've done throughout your life. He is faithful to forgive and to cleanse.

If you're struggling for the words, you can say, "Jesus, I know that I've sinned, and I'm sorry for those sins." Take some time here to name them specifically to Him. "Please forgive me for _____. I believe that You died on a cross for my sins. Please forgive me for those sins, come into my heart and into my life, and cleanse me from all of that. I want You to be the Lord of my life from now on." That's it! It's very simple! Jesus not only died, but He also rose from the dead three days later (Mark 14-16). He overcame the power of sin and death. This means that now, with His help and His Spirit inside of you (this comes into you as you invite Him in), you also can overcome sin or anything else that comes your way. How exciting and wonderful! And it's all free to us! Jesus' precious blood paid the price for us!

If you've just prayed that prayer, I am so, so happy for you, and I want to be the first one to welcome you into your new family – God's family.

I encourage you to get a Bible and begin reading it every day. Don't feel overwhelmed by the size of it. Just ask God to show you where to read and ask Him to help you understand it, and He will! Also, ask Him how to get connected with other believers in your area. He will lead you one step and one day at a time. God bless you!

Other titles by this author:

*I Found God Outside of Church*

*Pain-Free Periods: Yes, It Is Possible!*

www.ingramcontent.com/pod-product-compliance
Lightning Source LLC
Chambersburg PA
CBHW050241120526
44590CB00016B/2181